Century Tower, University of Florida.
Inset, Albert and Alberta, top gators.

Published by
LONGSTREET PRESS, INC.
A subsidiary of Cox Newspapers,
A subsidiary of Cox Enterprises, Inc.
2140 Newmarket Parkway
Suite 118
Marietta, GA 30067

Printed in the United States of America

1st printing 1996

Library of Congress Catalog Card
Number: 96-76503

ISBN 1-56352-331-0

Book design by Graham and Company
Graphics

Electronic Film output and separation by
Overflow Graphics Inc. Forest Park, GA

Jacket design by Neil Hollingsworth

GATOR GREATNESS

A Photo Anthology of Sports
at the University of Florida

FOREWORD by Norm Carlson

with Special Introductory Remarks from
Dr. John Lombardi, President
The University of Florida
and
Jeremy Foley, Director of Athletics
The University of Florida
and
a Special Commentary from
Steve Spurrier, Head Football Coach
The University of Florida

Edited by Philip L. Ben

Photo Credits

[Credits Legend: T=top; B=bottom; C=center; L=left; R=right.]

All-Sport: p. 23T, 25 (photo by Otto Greule), 90 (photo by Otto Gruele), 97BR, 102 (photos by Tony Duffy); Carlson, Norm: p. 8; Florida Designs, Inc.: p. 16 (artwork by Harry Michael); Hoby Cards, Inc.: p. 9B, 58B; Montgomery Art Company: p. 32 (artwork by Michael Montgomery); Time, Inc.: 145B, 158; University Athletic Association Marketing & Promotions Department: p. 7; University of Florida Archives: p. 24R, 26, 28, 34, 35, 36-37T, 37B (from the Florida Alumnus, University of Florida Alumni Association, November 1929), 38-44, 46, 47T, 51B, 52-53, 54B, 56-57, 66, 69, 70, 73BL and BR, 75B, 116BR; University of Florida News & Public Affairs: p. 1, 11T, 51T (photo by Herb Press), 150-151; University of Florida Sports Information Office: p. 6, 9T, 9B, 10, 11B, 12, 13 (photo by Andy Windham), 14 (photo by Al Messerschmidt), 15TL, 15TR (photo by James Stephens), 15B, 17 (photo by UF News & Public Affairs), 18-19, 20, 21T (photo by Gene Bednarek), 21B (photo by Jeff Gage), 22 (photos by Larry Pierce), 23B, 24L, 27B, 29L (photo by Jeff Gage), 29R (photo by Michael Holohan), 30 (photo by Reggie Grant), 31, 36B, 45, 47B, 48-50, 54T, 55, 57, 58T, 60-65, 67, 68, 71, 72-73, 73T, 74 (photo by Michael Holohan), 75T, 76, 77T, 77B (photo by John Moran, The Gainesville Sun), 78-84, 85TL, 85TR (photo by Adrian Dennis), 85BL, 85BR (photo by Fred Vance), 86TL and 86B, 86TR (photo by Fred Vance), 87T (photo by Eugene Burton), 87BL, 87BR (photo by Kevin Higley), 88, 89TL (photo by Stephen Morton), 89TR, 89B (photo by Tom Warren), 91T, 91B (photo by Kathy Cafazzo), 92 (photo by Quinten Stevens), 93T (photo by Greg Oell), 93C (photo by Tim Morse), 93B (photo by Jeff Gage), 94 (inset photos BL and BR by Adrian Dennis), 95 (photo by Allen Cheuvront), 96L, 97R (photo by James Stephens), 97T (photo by James Stephens), 97BL (photo by Tom Warren), 98-99, 99B (photo by Hugh Harling), 100-101, 103T, 103C (photo by C.W. Pack Sports), 103B, 104T (photo by Ron Irby), 104B (photo by Brenda Handy), 105, 106 (photo by Patrick Murphy-Racey), 107T, 107B (photo by Jeff Gage), 108 (photos by Eileen Connors), 109, 109B (photo by James Stephens), 110-111 (photos by Jason Davis), 112TL (photo by Ann Schwaller), 112C (photo by UPI), 112BL, 112BR (photo by Bruce Fine), 113T (photo by Tim Davis), 113BL and BR, 114, 115T (photo by Kevin Wisniewski), 115B (photo by Action Sports), 116TL and TR, 116BL, 117 (BL photo by Michael Holohan), 118-119, 120T, 120B (photo by Herb Press), 121, 122T, 122B (photo by Tim Morse), 123T (photo by Ron Irby), 123C and 123B, 124-128, 130L (photo by Roby Page), 130R (photo by Jeff Gage), 130L (photo by Roby Page), 130R, 132L (photo by Al Messerschmidt), 132R (photo by Art Seitz), 133-136, 137T (photo by Bruce Fine), 137B, 138, 139L, 139R (photo by Doug Opfer), 140-141, 140B (photo by C.W. Pack Sports), 142-144, 145T, 146-148, 149T (photo by Bruce Fine), 149B, 152T (photo by Sean Meyers), 152B, 153, 154, 155 (photo by Roby Page), 156, 157 (photo by Jeff Gage), 159, 160.

"Florida Gator," above, *by Michael Montgomery. Limited Edition prints available.*
For information, call 800/782-3216.

GATOR GREAT-NESS

Dear Gator Friends:

It is great to be a Florida Gator! In the classrooms and on the playing fields, in the laboratories and in the arenas, in the libraries and on the tracks, the University of Florida enjoys the best of both worlds. In academics and athletics, Florida ranks among the very best universities in the nation.

Our athletic program thrives because of the quality of our student athletes, the dedication and commitment of our coaching staff, the organizational and financial leadership in the University Athletic Association and especially because of the great support of our students, alumni, friends, fans and other members of the university family. The success of our athletic program brings national and international recognition and generates millions in financial support to enhance our academic programs and provide a better quality of life for our students.

Gone are the days of "wait until next year." Gone are the days of "it's hard to be a Gator." Now we can hardly wait until the next year and it truly is great to be a Florida Gator.

Our fans have learned to ask before they act and provide the best support in the world. Thank you.

Sincerely yours,

Dr. John Lombardi,
President, University
of Florida.

Fellow Gators:

As someone who has been affiliated with the University of Florida athletic program since 1976, I'm very proud to be part of one of the nation's finest athletic programs. We have tremendous coaches, athletes, facilities and support staff. And now we have an outstanding publication to capture some of the memorable moments in our history. Turn these pages and enjoy our national champions, SEC champions and All-Americans . . . our leaders in the community and our leaders of the country . . . the coaching staff and administration that have made it happen. This picturebook is for all of those people who have helped make the University of Florida what it is today, and this book is also for you — the Gator fans . . .

Jeremy Foley,
Director of Athletics,
University of Florida.

Enjoy!

UNIVERSITY OF FLORIDA
The Best of Both Worlds

Florida's 654 total SEC Academic Honor Roll selections since 1981 leads the SEC. Its 216 total honorees the past three years is the best three-year total in league history and its 74 selections for the 1992-93 academic year set a SEC single-season record.

An independent research study, published in the June 1992 *NCAA News*, named the University of Florida one of the nation's six premier schools for having the best mix of academic quality and athletic success. Penn State, Southern Cal, Stanford, Texas and UCLA joined Florida in the elite group which was determined by comparing rankings of the nation's top academic institutions and athletic success over a 10-year period (1982-1991).

Florida is the only member school of the Association of American Universities, the most prestigious organization in higher education, to have its football team ranked in the top 10 in the final AP Poll in each of the past four seasons.

ACADEMICS

- Ranks among the top three schools in the nation for the number of academic programs offered on a single campus.

- A 1994 study by *U.S. News and World Report* ranks UF fourth among all schools in the nation for "Best Values".

- Ranks fourth among public institutions, and eighth among all institutions, in the number of new National Merit Scholars enrolled in 1994.

- Ranks second nationally among public institutions, and eighth among all institutions, in the number of new National Achievement Scholars enrolled in 1994.

- A national report by the Council To Aid Education ranks UF third among all public institutions for alumni support.

- Ranks third nationally among all U.S. universities in patents issued, and among the top five in revenue from royalties.

- One of only 60 of the more than 1,200 colleges and universities in the nation that belongs to the Association of American Universities — the most prestigious organization for higher education in North America.

- Home to national research centers in science, medicine and engineering.

ATHLETICS

- Its overall program has ranked as one of the top 10 in national all-sport rankings in each of the past 12 years, including a top-five ranking in each of the past six years.

- Along with UCLA, UF is the only school in the nation to finish in the top 10 in the national all-sport rankings each year since 1984.

- Captured the Southeastern Conference All-Sports Championship seven of the past eight years.

- Became the first school in SEC history to capture both the men's and women's all-sport titles in the same year (1992), a feat it also accomplished in 1993.

- Captured 75 SEC titles since 1980, the top total in the league, including a record eight SEC titles in 1991-92.

- One of just five schools to be ranked among the nation's 10 finest in both men's and women's sports in a 1994 vote by Div. 1-A Athletic Directors.

- Since 1980, its teams have combined to finish the season in the top 10 in their respective sports 116 times, including 51 appearances in the final national top three.

- In the last six Olympic Games, 74 Gator student-athletes have won a combined total of 49 medals, including 25 gold. In the 1992 Summer Olympics, 25 Gators won 13 medals, including eight golds.

UNIVERSITY OF FLORIDA

FOREWORD

by Norm Carlson

Coverage of intercollegiate athletics at the University of Florida has never been lacking from the day the first alligator emblem appeared in owner Phillip Miller's sundries shop near campus in 1908 through the baseball team's heroic bid for a national championship, and the women's tennis team winning one, in 1996.

For 90 years almost every news angle has been used to bring the story of intercollegiate athletics to students, faculty, alumni and boosters, all of them important to Gators everywhere. However, the thought of a pictorial review of the total program is an idea which didn't find its time until this book.

The story told by this photographic journey through the rich history of the Florida athletic program is exciting and nostalgic. Remember:

Finally, that first SEC football championship; Tracy Caulkins, the greatest female swimmer of all time; Clyde (Cannonball) Crabtree, who could punt with either foot and pass with either hand; Steve Spurrier, Heisman winner to head coach. Neal Walk, basketball All-American; the Final Four team. Steve O'Connell, boxing champion to university president. national championship teams and individ-

Norm Carlson, Assistant Athletic Director for Communications, University of Florida, and Gator source-authority.

uals; football's "Fergie" Ferguson who, along with so many others, made the greatest sacrifice for his country in war.

The people pictured on these pages make you proud to be a Gator . . . from Major James A. Van Fleet to Coach Andy Brandi . . . from Dr. John J. Tigert to Dr. John Lombardi . . . administrators like Ruth Alexander and Ann Marie Rogers and Jeremy Foley . . . athletes like Danny Wuerffel. They help us define and remember the excellence upon which the Florida program has been built by coaches, athletes and administrators alike.

These pages bring back memories of champions, All-Americans, Hall of Famers, Olympians, record-breakers and glorious moments of accomplishment in all sports in which Gators compete, and we can relive them with pride. This book by Philip Ben is a tribute to the tradition of the Orange-and-Blue. It recalls a wonderful period in the lives of all of us who developed a strong bond with our university.

Whether your fondest memories come from time spent in Alligator Alley, Ben Hill Griffin Stadium or just plain Florida Field, Perry Field, the O'Connell Center, Florida Pool, Scott Linder Stadium, University Golf Course, Percy Beard Track or the old cinder track, these pictures are worth savoring.

My personal devotion goes back to a fall afternoon in 1952

HARVARD, AHOY!
Here Come Those Florida Alligators

GOODBREAD

CRABTREE

VAN SICKLE

CAWTHON

They're Real, Live Alligators!

By HOWARD E. FILL
Central Press Sport Correspondent.
GAINESVILLE, Oct. 30.—For the

when Buford Long, Rick Casares and Charlie LaPradd led a Gator team to Jacksonvillle to soundly beat Georgia, 30-0, setting the stage for the first-ever Florida appearance in a post-season football bowl game. I was hooked, and still am 45 years later.

But this book is about more than football, It is about an athletic program which proudly represents a great university, and the men and women who have made it so worthwhile.

CHARLIE LaPRADD

REFLECTIONS OF A GATOR GREAT . . .

Steve Spurrier

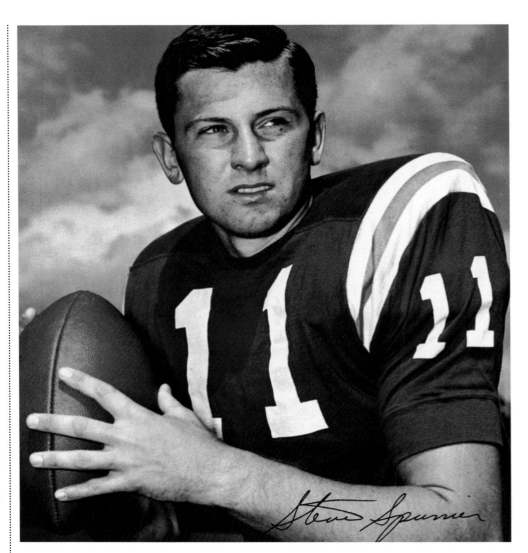

I enrolled at the University of Florida as a freshman in the fall of 1963, and people have asked me why I came here.

As a high school player, coming out of Johnson City, Tennessee, I really didn't know where to go to college. I wanted to go somewhere in the Southeastern Conference, and I visited several places . . . Alabama, Ole Miss, Vanderbilt, Kentucky, Tennessee. The University of Tennessee was still playing the old single wing offense my senior year, and that was not best for me as a high school quarterback and, hopefully, a future college quarterback.

I didn't visit Florida until after our high school basketball season was over. Came down here in late March. The weather was nice; Coach Graves really showed a tremendous interest in me, recruited me hard and convinced us that he would look after me while I was here, which he certainly did. So, he was a big factor. And a big factor, too, was that one of the coaches said you ought to go to school in the state you'd like to live in. I figured there's got to be a reason that people save their money their whole lives to retire in Florida — it's a nice place to live. So, I had an opportunity to go to school here, play ball in the Southeastern Conference and possibly live here afterwards. With all of that together, and Coach Graves, influence, this seemed to be the best place for me.

In my three years as a varsity player, we had a lot of victories . . . but no championships. I remember several games that we won in

the last moments. The Auburn game where I was able to kick a field goal in the last couple of minutes to beat 'em 30-27; a game we had with FSU that we threw a touchdown with about a minute and a half left to win. I remember those well. But then there are some games that we lost that knocked us out of the championships. I remember those just as much as the victories.

We went to the Sugar Bowl and the Orange Bowl during my three years, and two of those three years we were one game away from winning the SEC championship, but we checked up a game short each year. Hopefully, that has helped me as a coach, to understand the importance of maintaining the level of intensity

Footsteps to follow. Florida star running back Emmitt Smith (1987-89) poses with portrait of the1966 Heisman Trophy winner at New York's Downtown Athletic Club in1989. Smith was a finalist in the ballotting for the '89 Heisman.

that it takes to win championships . . . to try, as a coach, to get every team to achieve the most it's capable of achieving each year.

I was fortunate enough to win the Heisman Trophy my senior year, and I was honored to receive it . . . it's one of the top awards that an amateur athlete can receive. I tried to share the honor with my team. But individual awards are difficult to share, whereas, when you win a championship you've all won it. That's why I think winning championships for your team is much more important than individual awards — being able to share an accomplishment like a championship

with a group because you can all be a part of something special.

When I came back here to the University of Florida as head football coach, I was excited about the possibility of being able to accomplish some things that hadn't been done before. We hadn't quite achieved what we could, potentially, in football. We're the largest school in the Southeastern Conference, the high school talent in this state may be the best, we fill the stands with 85,000 fans each home game; this is the kind of situation that you'd like to go into anywhere . . . where the potential is there to accomplish a lot of things. It wasn't just

because I'm an alumnus of this school that I was excited and fortunate to be coming back here. I saw it as an opportunity to coach at one of the best schools in the country. Period.

In football, as in life, the most important thing is to develop the "habit of success." As coaches we try to develop that "habit of success" so that, year after year, you get your players into that attitude where they expect good things to happen. We're in that frame of mind now here at Florida, where we believe we're supposed to do well. And I'm proud that we've got it going now, that we strive to meet our potential, achieve the most that we're capable of, year after year.

A TRADITION OF CHAMPIONS

Gator basketball standout Andrew DeClercq celebrates the moment as Florida captures the Eastern Regional championship at the Miami Arena and heads to the NCAA Final Four in Charlotte, UF's first trip to the Final Four.

Above left, the 1996 Florida women's tennis team offers up a "Gator Chomp" in Tallahassee after capturing the NCAA championships, hosted by Florida State. *Left*, Gator pitcher ace John Burke (1990-92) sets to fire a fastball home at the 1991 College Baseball World Series. *Above right*, the picture of poise and grace, UF gymnast Elfi Schlegel (1983-86).

As the followers of the Orange-and-Blue will tell you, from Miami to the Panhandle ...

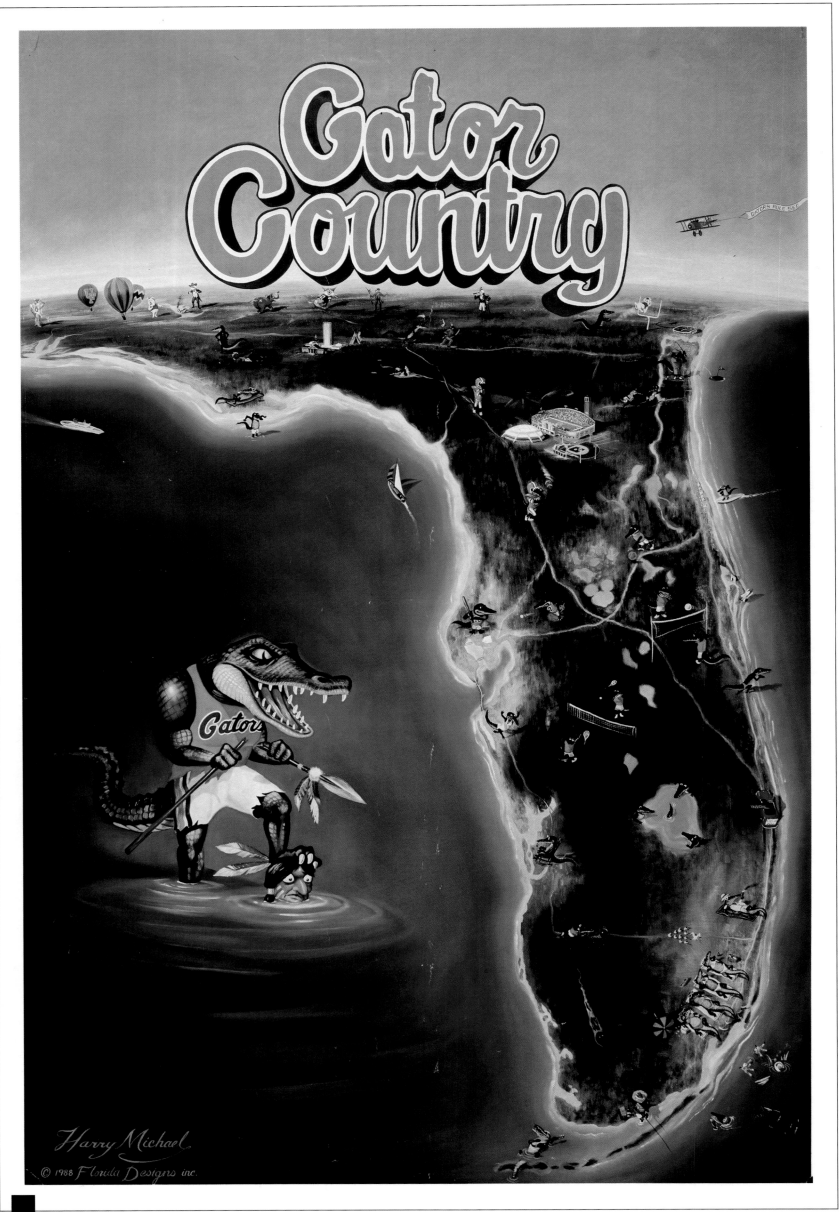

Heeeeeere come the Gators!

. . . this is Gator Country.

A golden moment for Florida swimming, the 1984 Los Angeles Olympics, where UF swimmers took 19 medals, including 13 gold. *Below,* five Gator gold medalists, left to right, David Larson, Theresa Andrews, Mary Wayte, Tracy Caulkins and Mike Heath.

And today, more than ever, the Gators' domain extends far beyond the boundaries of the State of Florida, across the nation . . .

UF swimming great Nicole Haislett, *left*, who captured three gold medals — in the 200-meter freestyle, the 400-meter free relay and the 400-meter medley relay — at the 1992 Barcelona Olympic Games . . . with a little encouragement from the folks back home, *below,* on the "34th Street Wall."

Facing page, Gator great Dennis Mitchell, a three-time Olympian, at Seoul, Barcelona and Atlanta.

The parade of Gator champions, at times, has seemed endless . . . and the sky the limit. Sometimes, not even that. *Above*, Mike Holloway, up, up and away at the 1992 NCAA Outdoor Track-and-Field Championships. Holloway is the only four-time SEC pole vaulting champion in history.

Florida trackster Michelle Freeman, *above left*, hurdled her way to victory in the 1992 NCAA 100-meter finals, and Monifa Taylor, *far right,* took the 1993 NCAA 55-meter hurdles title. The crowning achievement for the Lady Gator track team came in 1992 with the NCAA indoor team title.

Tom Slade established the trend, *inset right*, winning the individual championship of the old Southern Conference, the forerunner of the SEC, in 1924. And Florida men's and women's tennis players and teams have continued the tradition over the years, with a spate of individual and team titles at the conference and national levels. Among UF's most recent title-winners,1993 NCAA men's doubles champions Mark Merklein and David Blair, *above left*.

The 1992 women's tennis team, coached by Andy Brandi and led by Lisa Raymond, *front row, center,* was perfection defined: 30-0 on the season, 14-0 in the SEC, and SEC and NCAA champions. Raymond captured the 1992 NCAA women's singles crown and repeated in '93.

In 1924 the Gainesville Golf and Country Club — today's University Golf Course — opened with nine holes, and the UF golf team, *above,* toured those nine holes, as has every men's and women's golf team of the university since. A second nine holes were added to the course in 1934, and the parade of collegiate and professional golfing legends who have traversed those grounds in the 60-plus years since has been phenomenal, among them Florida's 1968 NCAA men's championship team, *opposite page, top,* and the 1986 NCAA women's champions, *opposite page, bottom,* featuring Page Dunlap, the 1986 NCAA women's medalist *(back row, center).*

The University of Florida volleyball team of 1923.

In the 1920s volleyball
at Florida was a guy thing . . .

Martha Ryans, *above right*, one of the early stars of the Florida volleyball program, established a school record of 372 career blocks during her four years (1985-88), a tally that still stands second on the all-time career list. Gudula Staub, *above left,* earned All-American accolades in 1991 and again in '92, and was named 1992 SEC Player of the Year.

but, today, the name of the game . . .

The day, say many, that Florida's volleyball program came of age . . . was the day in 1991 when the Lady Gators served up a five-game victory over LSU, the defending SEC champion and then ranked #5 in the nation. The Florida volleyballers went on to a 35-5 season's mark and an NCAA bid.

. . . has changed!

The powerful 1992 volleyball team, top, rolled to a 34-2 record, the SEC crown (with a perfect 14-0 mark) and the NCAA Final Four with three All-Americans in its ranks: Heidi Anderson *(at the right in the front row)*, Gudula Staub *(front row, third from the left)* and freshman stand-out Aycan Gokberk *(back row, fourth from the left)*. The '92 contingent added 14 victories to a homecourt winning streak that had begun in 1990 and reached an NCAA-record 56 straight wins before the streak ended in 1994.

©1991 Michael Montgomery

THE CHRONOLOGY

THE EARLY DAYS

Gators have always been a big part of the Florida scene. Never more so than today. And if the Gators rule the Florida fens, from the Panhandle to the Keys and all points in between, then it is in Gainesville — on the courts and playing fields of the University of Florida — where they hold sway.

The sons and daughters, Gators and Lady Gators, of the university have represented themselves and their university proudly and well over the past 90 years . . . throughout the State of Florida, across the nation, and around the world, across the full range of athletic endeavor — from soccer to football, cross-country to track-and-field, basketball to baseball, swimming, golf, tennis and volleyball.

Herein, then, lies the story, in pictures and prose, of the athletes and coaches — each and every one, in their own right, "Gator Greats" — who have contributed to "Gator Greatness" and the greatness of one of America's premier universities — the University of Florida.

The "Gator" became a part of the University of Florida and Florida athletics in 1907 when Phillip Miller, who owned a Gainesville drug and sundries store, ordered a set of banners and pennants from the Michie Company of Charlottesville, Virginia to sell to Florida students who frequented his shop. When the Michie manager inquired as to what the UF mascot was, so that the logo might appear on the pennants, Miller realized the University had no mascot. His son, Austin, suggested the alligator, since it was indigenous to the State of Florida; the Michie manager seconded the notion, since it would be unique among all colleges and universities in the nation, and the idea — and the nickname — stuck. The "Gator" banners and pennants appeared in the window of Miller's drug store in the fall of 1908, and the Florida Fighting Gators took to the athletic fields that fall with a new nickname . . . and a lasting legacy.

The first football team of the consolidated University of Florida at Gainesville took to the gridiron in the fall of 1906, downing the Gainesville Athletic Club, 16-6, en route to a 5-3-0 season. In 1907, the Florida footballers, *bottom right*, continued their winning ways and finished the season with a record of 4-1-1.

The early days of Florida football ranged from "Commodore Corbett" to "Major Van Fleet." The man who scored the winning touchdown against the Columbia Athletic Club in 1907 was team captain Roy W. Corbett, *facing page*, who also happened to be the first student to enroll at the consolidated University of Florida in September, 1906. Corbett went on to a distinguished career at sea, retiring with the rank of Commodore. James A. Van Fleet, *above*, who headed up the University ROTC program in the early 1920s and '30s, also headed up the Florida football program in 1923 and '24, with a record of 12 wins, 3 losses and 4 ties, including two ties with powerful Georgia Tech and a 16-6 win over Alabama at Birmingham. Militarily, Van Fleet served with distinction in both World Wars and commanded the U.S. Eighth Army in Korea, rising to the rank of general.

FLORIDA 1928 NATIONAL HIG

The 1928 football season marked a major turning point in the evolution of Florida football, from its humble beginnings at the start of the century to national prominence. The '28 Fighting Gators, above, the highest scoring team in the nation that season (averaging 37.3 points per game), thundered to an 8-1-0 mark, and featured Florida's first All-American and future Hall-of-Famer, end Dale Vansickel, *left,* who went on to a career as one of Hollywood's top movie stuntmen.

SCORING CHAMPIONS 336-44

With team captain Rainey Cawthon riding herd, *right,* the Gators of '29 rolled to an 8-2-0 record, including a 20-6 win over Oregon in an intersectional matchup in Miami at season's end.

In the early days, the football team was not the only crew that was "fleet-of-foot," as evidenced by the track team of 1910, *above.* Official records in track and field were kept from 1923 on and, *left,* the Gators were off-and-running, garnering glory for Alma Mater, *opposite page.*

MID-CENTURY

In the early 1930s, riding the tide of success from the late '20s, Florida football entered a new era. Florida Field, *above*, became the home of the Gator gridders. The stadium, which originally consisted of the lower section of today's Ben Hill Griffin Stadium, was dedicated on November 8, 1930, in memory of Florida's war dead, in a game with Alabama. Over the years Florida Field became a comfortable fen for the Fighting Gators . . . and a den of death for wary visitors.

The football team was not the only team with the horses at Florida in the '30s. The University polo team, *above*, rode the boards from the late '20s until the outbreak of World War II, taking on private polo clubs and other university teams throughout the South — and attracting quite a fan following.

In the fall of 1935, a senior cager from Miami who had displayed a good deal of athleticism and considerable leadership ability was elected team captain for the 1935-36 basketball season. George Smathers ably captained the '36 roundballers, completed his undergraduate work at the University and went on to the Florida College of Law . . . and from there on to a distinguished career of public service, including 19 years as U.S. Senator for the State of Florida, from 1950 to 1969. Smathers retired from the Senate to private law practice in Miami in 1969, but his sense of public service and involvement continued. In 1991 he gave a $20 million endowment to the University of Florida Libraries, one of the largest private donations ever made to an institution of higher learning in the United States. The libraries of the university were renamed the George A. Smathers libraries of the University of Florida, *opposite page*, in acknowledgment of Smathers' generosity and years of service to the State and its people.

With the outbreak of World War II, life changed dramatically at the university, as it did throughout the state of Florida, the nation and the world. The University of Florida made a valuable contribution to the American initiative in the Second World War, and in Korea, by sending one of its own — Major James Van Fleet — into the fray. As noted earlier Van Fleet coached the Gator gridders with distinction in 1923 and '24, and in World War II and Korea, he served his nation with distinction militarily, being honored with not one, but two New York ticker-tape parades upon his return from those conflicts. Van Fleet's Eighth Infantry Regiment spearheaded the 4th Division assault landing at Utah Beach in the Normandy invasion on D-Day, June 6, 1944. And, during the Korean conflict, Lieutenant General Van Fleet commanded the U.S. Eighth Army. He retired in March, 1953, with the permanent rank of full general.

Another of the university's own who served his Alma Mater well athletically and served his nation greatly in war was Forrest K. "Fergie" Ferguson, *above,* an All-American end in football, the Florida state collegiate boxing champion and, in 1942, the winner of the National AAU javelin crown. Ferguson entered World War II as a second lieutenant in '42 and served with distinction until he was critically wounded during the Normandy Invasion, a campaign of which, coincidentally, Florida's James Van Fleet served as a commander. Ferguson, who was awarded the Distinguished Service Cross for heroism under fire, eventually died of his war wounds, but he was immortalized in the annals of Florida athletics for his personal athletic achievements and by the Forrest K. Ferguson Award, presented annually to the senior football player who demonstrates outstanding leadership, character and courage.

Baseball has been a part of the Florida athletic scene since the early days. The baseball team of 1912 compiled a record of 8-3-1 and laid claim to the title of "Florida State Champions." By the 1920s, Florida baseball was having an extraordinary impact on the sport nationwide, sending a plethora of talent into the major leagues. The 1927 team, *above,* had five major leaguers in its midst with a phenomenal combined 24 years in the majors: pitcher Henry Boney *(back row, second from the left),* shortstop John Burnett *(front row, second from the right),* pitcher and team captain James "Tiny" Chaplin *(back row, third from the right, and in the artwork at the left),* pitcher Ned Porter *(front row, third from the left)* and outfielder Lance Richbourg *(front row, center, and in the photograph at the left).*

In 1948 Dave Fuller assumed the baseball head coaching position at Florida, the beginning of 28 years for him as skipper of the UF diamond program . . . 28 years, 557 victories and three SEC championships — the first brought home by the '52 crew, *above*. His tenure also produced three NCAA bids, five All-Americans and eight major leaguers. One Florida major leaguer of the day, Al Rosen, *right*, played his college ball at Gainesville in 1941-42 and launched his ten years as a player in the majors in 1947.

MOST VALUABLE PLAYER — 1953
AMERICAN LEAGUE

AL ROSEN

Among the brightest stars of the Dave Fuller coaching era were first baseman Perry McGriff, *above,* a Gator gridder, who garnered All-American honors for his baseball prowess in 1959, and third baseman Tom Moore, *left,* who led Florida to the NCAA tournament in 1960 and again in 1962, and earned All-American accolades for himself in '62 and '63. Moore set a school record of 26 stolen bases in his junior year and returned as a senior to snare 20 more stolen bags and lead the Gators in hitting with a .357 batting average.

Success was not limited to baseball at UF in the '50s. Football enjoyed considerable success under Coach Bob Woodruff, *above left,* with two-sport man Haywood Sullivan. Woodruff led Florida to its first two postseason bowl appearances, the Gator Bowl (where else?) in 1952 and again in 1958, and the Gators gave plenty of folks hell on the gridiron from 1950 to 1959. three of Woodruff's gridders earned first-team All-American accolades: tackle Charlie LaPradd (1952), guard John Barrow (1956) and tackle Vel Heckman (1958).

THE SIXTIES & SEVENTIES

Gator football entered one of its most exciting and successful eras in the 1960s — the Ray Graves era. With Graves and his charges came thrills, chills and victory — none more electrifying than Florida's 10-6 win over Bear Bryant's Alabama Crimson Tide in Tuscaloosa in 1963, *above*, a victory that earned the ebullient Graves a ride off the turf of Denny Stadium. Under Graves, the Gators garnered 70 wins, against but 31 losses and 4 ties, from 1960 to 1969, and earned five bowl bids, Graves retired at the end of the 1969 season to devote his attentions to the university's athletic directorship.

With 33 seconds left to play in the 1960 Georgia Tech game, half-back Lindy Infante, *inset*, crashed over the goal line. First-year coach Ray Graves opted for the then-new two-point conversion, the Gators were victorious and history had been made. UF had served notice that it was going to be tough to hold the Gators during the decade of the '60s. Indeed . . . it was.

Graves' Gators battered Georgia, 22-14, in 1960 before a Gator Bowl stadium record crowd of 48,622. Florida found the confines of the Gator Bowl so friendly that it returned at season's end to the Gator Bowl postseason classic and another victory, this time over Baylor, capping a 9-2 season.

The '60s was an All-Star-spangled era for Florida football, with 33 All-SEC selections and 11 All-Americans, among them: fullback Larry Dupree (1962-64), riding in style, *above*.

Another football All-American of the era was end Charlie Casey, *above left and inset,* a two-sport man at Florida and Kodak All-American in 1965. One other notable in the plethora of Gator grid All-Americans of the '60s included center and future UF athletic director Bill Carr (1964-66), *top right.*

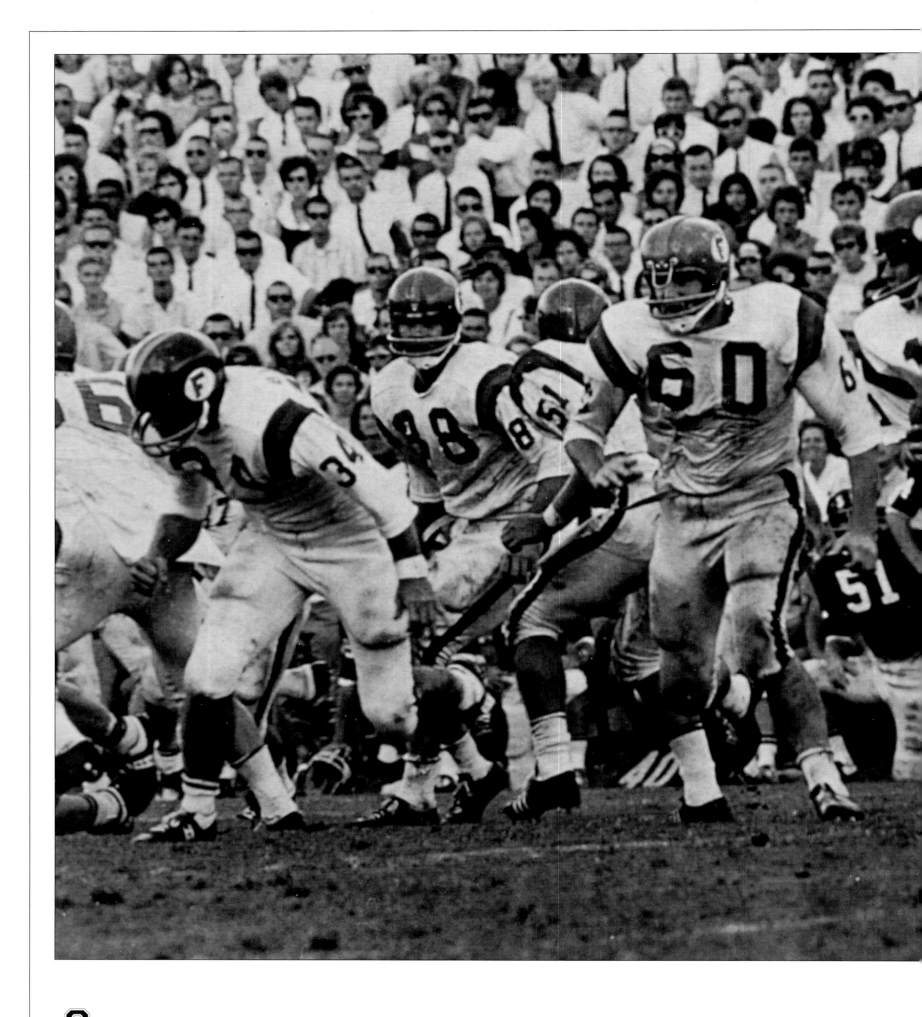

One of the most lauded and laureled players of the Graves era, or any era of Florida football, was two-time All-American and 1966 Heisman Trophy winner Steve Spurrier, *above,* who quarterbacked the Gators to the Sugar Bowl in 1965 and the Orange Bowl in 1966. Spurrier and All-American fullback Larry Smith, *right*, spearheaded Florida's win over Georgia Tech in the Orange Bowl. Smith's 94-yard touchdown run, an Orange Bowl record, in the third quarter broke open a close game, and Spurrier ably engineered the Gators over the Techmen, 27-12.

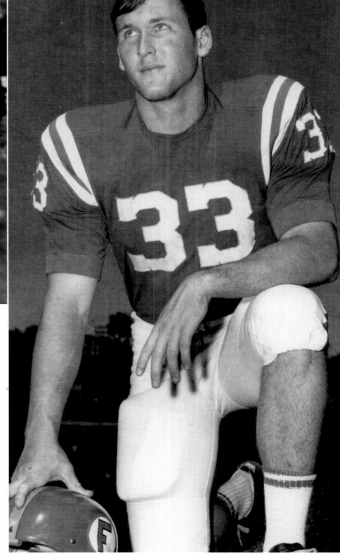

JOHN REAVES

The Gators were flying high by the end of the '60s. With All-American flanker Carlos Alvarez hauling in passes from quarterback John Reaves, the Gators soared to a 9-1-1 season in 1969, highlighted by a win over Tennessee in the Gator Bowl. Alvarez set school records for pass receptions (88) and receiving yardage (1,329) that year that still stand today. And fellow "Super Soph" John Reaves began his march toward All-American honors (in 1971) and becoming the NCAA's all-time leading passer, with 7,581 career yards. Fittingly enough, the NCAA record-breaking pass came against Miami in the Orange Bowl in the 1971 season's finale, *above,* Reaves-to-Alvarez.

All-SEC running back Tommy Durrance (#33), *above,* with the hand-off from John Reaves (#7) hurtles into the end zone for the winning touchdown against Tulane in Tampa in 1969. A Reaves-to-Alvarez two-point conversion, *left,* sealed the victory for the Gators.

The Gator Bowl in Jacksonville, always like a second home to the Gators from Gainesville, was an especially agreeable place to play for Florida in the '60s. The "World's Largest Cocktail Party," the annual Florida-Georgia game at the Gator Bowl, was particularly festive for UF followers. Florida dominated the series, with 6 wins and a tie against the 'Dogs. The Gators also participated in and won three Gator Bowl post-season classics during the decade, vs. Baylor in 1960 (13-12), Penn State in 1962 (17-7) and Tennessee in 1969 (14-13), the latter a great send-off for retiring head coach Ray Graves.

Ray Graves, above, on the eve of his coaching finale, readies his Saurians for their showdown with Tennessee in the 1969 Gator Bowl. Another "Gator Great" also hung up his whistle at the end of the 1969 season: Graves' top assistant and defensive coordinator, Gene Ellenson, right, a Graves assistant from 1960 to 1969 and later executive secretary of the Gator Boosters from 1974 until 1986 . . . in all 35 years of service to the university and its athletic program.

The end of the 1969 season brought with it the end of the Ray Graves era of Florida football. But important steps toward modern-day greatness for the UF football program had been taken, and it was '60s folk heroes like the "Super Sophs of '69" — *above, left to right,* John Reaves, Mike Rich, Tommy Durrance and Carlos Alvarez — who took those steps that put Florida football on the path to greatness in the modern era. Doug Dickey, with the "Super Sophs," *above,* succeeded Graves as head coach at the end of the '69 season. Through the '70s and '80s, a long journey lay ahead for Florida football, down a sometimes tortuous path, but it was a journey that would ultimately lead the Gator gridders to their greatest era ever in the 1990s; a journey that began in the '60s, when a fellow named Spurrier trod the turf of Florida Field in players' cleats . . . cleats he would someday trade in for coaches' shoes.

If offensive heroes of the late '60s and early '70s like John Reaves put opponents into a whirl, rock-ribbed defenders like defensive end Jack Youngblood, and linebacker Ralph Ortega, *left,* brought opponents to grinding halts. Youngblood was named All-American in 1970, and Ortega garnered All-American honors in 1974. Youngblood was honored as an "SEC Legend" at the 1995 SEC championship game in Atlanta, *above,* where his alma mater was making history, as well, successfully pursuing its third consecutive league crown.

The end of the 1960s and the beginning of the '70s saw the dawn of a new era for Florida athletically – and an important step forward – with the advent of the black athlete at UF. The contributions that black athletes have made to the university's athletic success since have been immeasurable. Ron Coleman, *left,* a long-and triple-jumper in track-and-field from 1968 to 1972, was Florida's first scholarship black athlete. And Willie Jackson, *right,* and Leonard George were the university's first black scholarship football players (1969-72). Jackson's sons followed in their father's footsteps – and jersey number. Willie, Jr., was a Gator gridder from 1990 to 1993, and brother Terry entered the university as a freshman in the fall of 1995 – all wearing the Orange-and-Blue #22 proudly and well . . . all in the family.

Change is sometimes slow in coming, but once change is implemented, progress is often swift. Within a few short years of Willie Jackson's arrival at the University of Florida, two outstanding black athletes — Sammy Green and Wes Chandler — were making their marks on the gridiron and earning All-American honors for their efforts. Green, *below,* alternated between nose guard and linebacker during his playing days, from 1972 to 1975, being named All-American linebacker in his senior year. And split end Wes Chandler, *left,* a two-time All-American (1976, '77), dazzled fans and foes alike with his pass-catching aerobatics from 1974 to 1977.

In 1950 former UF basketball center and team captain George Smathers (1934-36), *bottom left, second from the right,* was entering the U.S. Senate for the first time, and Florida's basketball Gators were entering their first full season in Florida Gym, which became affectionately known as "Alligator Alley." Bob Emrick, *above left*, one Gator marksman of the era, could light up the scoreboards. A four-year letterman (1953-57) and twice All-SEC, in 1955 and '56, Emrick finished his playing days as UF's all-time leading career scorer, a distinction he held until the late '60s, when Neal Walk rewrote the record books. Another two-time All-SEC selection from Florida during the '50s and a 1958 All-American was guard Joe Hobbs, dribbling down "the Alley," *right.*

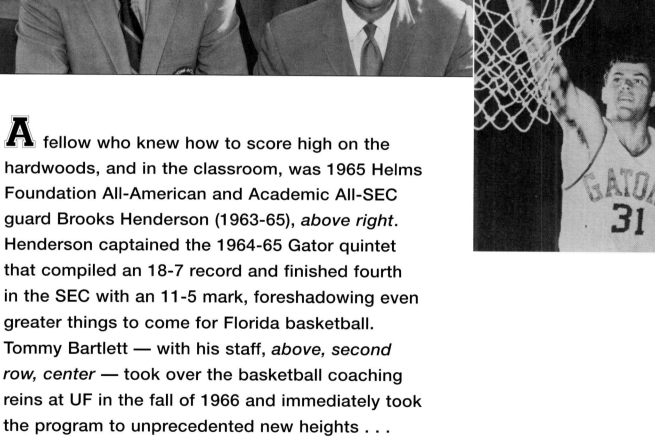

A fellow who knew how to score high on the hardwoods, and in the classroom, was 1965 Helms Foundation All-American and Academic All-SEC guard Brooks Henderson (1963-65), *above right*. Henderson captained the 1964-65 Gator quintet that compiled an 18-7 record and finished fourth in the SEC with an 11-5 mark, foreshadowing even greater things to come for Florida basketball. Tommy Bartlett — with his staff, *above, second row, center* — took over the basketball coaching reins at UF in the fall of 1966 and immediately took the program to unprecedented new heights . . . a 21-4 season and second place in the SEC. One of the moving forces behind the Gators surge to basketball prominence in 1966-67 was All-SEC center Gary Keller, *bottom right*, like Henderson an outstanding athlete and Academic All-SEC selection, as well.

Eager, willing and able to take over at the post position from Gary Keller upon his departure at the end of the 1966-67 season was a Miami product who would become the most honored player in Florida basketball history, Neal Walk, a two-time All-American (1968, '69) and the only Gator to have his basketball jersey (#41) retired. Walk's career point total of 1,600 broke Bob Emrick's career mark set in the 1950s and stood for more than a decade. Several of Walk's career marks still stand today, among them: scoring average (20.8 ppg), rebounds (1,181) and rebounding average (15.3). A first-round National Basketball Association draft choice, Walk went on to a successful career in the NBA with Phoenix, New Orleans and the New York Knickerbockers.

On an individual plane, center Neal Walk took over where Gary Keller had left off. And as a team, Florida built upon the momentum of the '67 quintet's success, momentum that carried the Gators to their first post-season basketball tournament appearance in 1969 at the National Invitation Tournament in New York's Madison Square Garden following an 18-9 season and a third-place finish in the SEC.

During the 1968-69 season and Florida's march to the NIT, sharp-shootin' junior forward Andy Owens, #45, *opposite page*, helped UF gun down Kentucky, 82-81, in "Alligator Alley" and went on, in 1969-70, to establish a Florida single-season scoring record of 27.0 points-per-game that still stands. During the 1971-72 season, the Gators paid another visit to Madison Square Garden, *above*, this time scoring a regular season victory over Army, 82-71.

In the early '80s, all-time UF career scorer Ronnie Williams, a four-time All-SEC selection (1981-84), needed little assistance in putting the ball through the hoop. Williams led his team in scoring all four of his years of varsity competition and finished with 2,090 career points.

The cozy confines of old Florida Gym, a.k.a. "Alligator Alley," *opposite page, right,* were friendly fens indeed for the basketball Gators from the 1949-50 season through the end of the 1979-80 campaign, and many an unwary foe was ambushed there. (Just ask the Kentucky teams of the late '60s, who lost three in a row in "the Alley.") But the growth of the university's student population and of the university's athletic programs, in particular basketball, swimming, track and gymnastics, called for a larger, multi-purpose facility on campus to accommodate student convocations and various social and athletic events. Toward that end the magnificent, futuristic, Stephen C. O'Connell Center, *above,* opened in the fall of 1980 with a 12,000-seat main arena for basketball, gymnastics and indoor track and a state-of-the-art natatorium for swimming.

West Palm Beach's Stephen C. O'Connell, UF Class of 1938 . . . a student leader and collegiate middleweight boxing champion, and future Florida College of Law graduate, Chief Justice of the Florida State Supreme Court and, *below right,* President of the University of Florida from 1967 to 1973.

The O'Connell Center Natatorium, home to Florida swimming and diving, has gained a reputation as one of the finest facilities in the country. It opened in January, 1981, replacing the wonderful but woefully impractical Florida Pool outdoor facility, and has hosted a string of prestigious regional and national events since, including the 1982 NCAA women's national championships, the men's SEC meets of 1981, '85 and '89 and the women's SEC competitions of 1984 and 1989.

The men's swim team of 1937, *above,* captured the inaugural SEC swimming and diving championship under head coach Frank Genovar and began a dynasty of dominance that has seen the Gators claim 33 league titles and two national championships in the years since. And long ago it was that coeds lounged by the side of old Florida Pool, *above right*, while the menfolk competed for regional, national and international honors. All that changed — and how — when the Lady Gators took the plunge into intercollegiate competition in 1972-73. Since the inception of the women's SEC swimming-and-diving championships in 1981, the Florida women have captured 15 of 16 league crowns and an NCAA championship, in 1982, and made an indelible mark for themselves and for the university, nationally and internationally.

Percy Beard, *above,* a former Olympic high hurdler and world record holder, established himself as a coaching legend at Florida from 1937 to 1964. His protegés were many and their legacy the foundation of modern-day Gator track-and-field greatness. Beard established the Florida Relays, which has become one of intercollegiate track's premier outdoor events, in the 1940s. *Right,* Earl Poucher, the 1954 NCAA pole vault champion.

A lasting memorial to a "Gator Great" and coaching legend: the Percy Beard Track & Field Complex . . .

. . . and, the magnificent O'Connell Center Indoor Track, a fitting monument to the legacy of Percy Beard, his protegés and the Florida track coaches and athletes who have followed.

JAMES SHAFFER (1961)
One All-America Honor

Shaffer advanced to the quarterfinals of the 1961 NCAA Championships before losing a hard-fought battle to California's William Hoogs, 9-7, 6-3. Shaffer's two points did give the Gators a tie for 10th place in the team standings. The southpaw from St. Petersburg, Fla. was a member of the Junior Davis Cup team. Shaffer won the SEC freshman individual title and posted a 46-12 varsity record. He was SEC individual titlist at No. 1 singles in 1961 and 1962, the first Gator to accomplish that feat.

Currently, Shaffer is an attorney with his own law firm, James A. Shaffer, P.A., Inc., in St. Petersburg.

BILL TYM (1963)
One All-America Honor

Tym advanced to the quarterfinals of the 1963 NCAA Championships before losing to eventual champion Dennis Ralston of USC, 6-2, 6-3. Tym's two points gave the Gators an 18th-place finish in the team standings.

The native of Lake Valhalla, N.J. captured the SEC individual title as a sophomore and junior at No. 2 and No. 1 singles, respectively. His career record was 41-9.

Tym was named head men's coach at Vanderbilt in 1987, and currently serves as Director of Tennis at the school. He is a past president and former executive director of the United States Professional Tennis Association.

Another "Gator Great" and coaching legend was Bill Potter, UF tennis coach from 1952 to 1977, with a record of 415 wins, against but 122 losses and 2 ties, five times SEC Coach of the Year, four SEC team titles and four All-Americans . . . the first James Shaffer, *above left,* in 1961 and Bill Tym, *above right*, two years later.

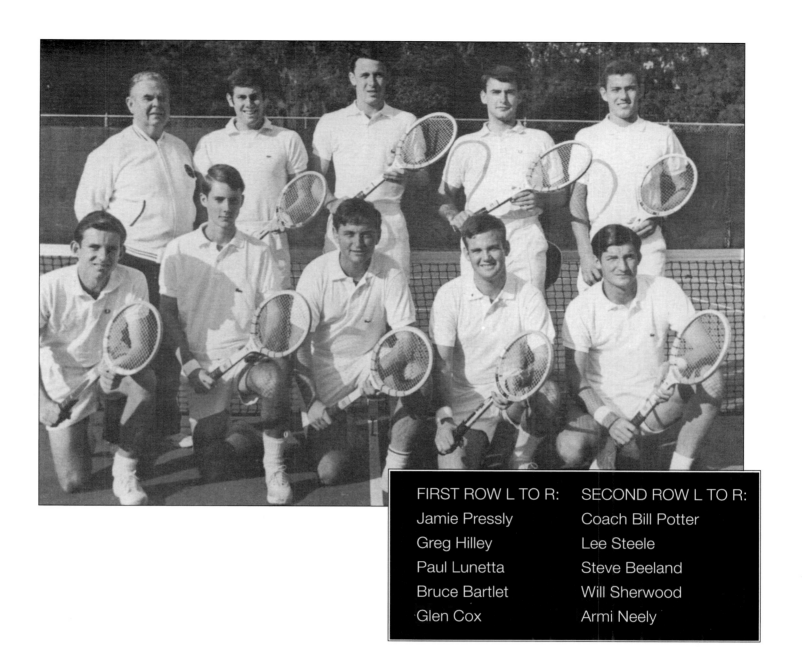

FIRST ROW L TO R:
Jamie Pressly
Greg Hilley
Paul Lunetta
Bruce Bartlet
Glen Cox

SECOND ROW L TO R:
Coach Bill Potter
Lee Steele
Steve Beeland
Will Sherwood
Armi Neely

One of the greatest Gator tennis teams of the Bill Potter era, indeed, one of the greatest Gator teams of all-time . . . the '68 contingent that rolled to a 23-1 mark and the SEC championship; in its ranks, two All-Americans, Armi Neely ('68, '69) and Jamie Pressly ('69).

Three Gator golfing greats and Professional Golfers Association tour veterans: *top left,* Dan Sikes (UF's first golf All-American, in 1952); Doug Sanders, *top right,* (who led the Gators to the 1955 SEC team title); and, *bottom center,* 1956 SEC medalist and All-American Dave Ragan.

Tommy Aaron

Youthful Tommy Aaron, Florida's first two-time SEC individual medalist (1957, '58), and Frank Beard, two-time All-American, in 1959 and again in 1960. Both went on to outstanding PGA tour careers, Aaron capturing the 1973 Master's title and Beard capping his career with Tournament of Champions victories in 1967 and '70.

Frank Beard

Bob Murphy, twice All-American (1965, '66), 1965 National Amateur champion and 1966 NCAA individual medalist while at Florida. In 1967 Murphy captured the Florida Open and launched a PGA career that made him a multimillionaire and a world-renowned figure in golf.

In 1968 the Gator golfers brought home their first NCAA team championship, and the next fall a freshman by the name of Andy North enrolled at UF, earning All-American honors three times (1970, '7l, '72) before his Gainesville golfing days were done. North went on to a distinguished PGA career, including winning two U.S. Opens, in 1978 and '85, and returned to Gainesville for a round from time-to-time, as at the 1978 Gator Golf Day, *right,* when another distinguished Florida alumnus and sometimes-golfer was in attendance . . . Steve Spurrier. *Above,* the 1973 golf team, the University's second NCAA championship team. In its ranks were All-Americans and future PGA tour members Phil Hancock, *second from the left;* Andy Bean, *second from the right*; and, *on the right,* Gary Koch, SEC medalist in 1973 and '74. Hancock picked up the initiative from Koch, taking SEC medalist honors in 1975 and '76.

Phil Hancock, *on the left*, three-time All-American at Florida (1974, '75, '76) and two-time SEC champion (1975, '76), along with the man that molded Hancock — and many others — into championship form: Buster Bishop, Gator men's golf mentor from 1974 to 1978. Bishop, three times SEC Coach of the Year, counted 25 All-Americans among his charges at Florida, and his teams brought home four SEC titles and two national championships, in 1968 and '73.

THE WOMEN'S PROGRAM

In 1969 Mimi Ryan, *left*, joined the faculty of Florida's College of Physical Education, Health and Recreation. During the 1970-71 school year, Ryan, a golf instructor, fashioned an intercollegiate golf "club" team out of talent drawn from the university's intramural program. In the spring of 1971 that club team captured the Florida State Women's Intercollegiate title, and won it again in the spring of 1972. Not entirely coincidentally, in the spring of 1972 the University of Florida Faculty Committee on Intercollegiate Athletics approved the establishment of an officially sanctioned intercollegiate athletic program for women at the university, and the UF women's intercollegiate program was born, with golf at the vangaurd of the movement.

And . . . as the old saying goes . . .

FLORIDA 25 WOMEN'S ATHLETICS

In the fall of 1972, the women's intercollegiate athletic program at the University of Florida was established . . . officially. Golf and tennis were already competing at the intercollegiate level on a "club" basis, with golf getting underway under the aegis of Mimi Ryan during the 1970-71 school year and tennis, coached by Linda Thornton of the College of Physical Education, Health and Recreation, entering into intercollegiate competition in the spring of 1972. Gymnastics, swimming and track-and-field were added to the officially-sanctioned lineup of women's sports during the 1972-73 school year, and four other sports were added over the next two years: basketball and cross-country in 1973-74; volleyball and softball in 1974-75. Softball was dropped in the spring of 1983, when the Association of Intercollegiate Athletics for Women (AIAW) folded and the NCAA failed to pick up softball as a nationally-sanctioned sport. Softball is due to return to the women's intercollegiate program at Florida in 1997, joining the other eight existing sports, including the most recent addition to lineup: soccer, which kicked off its inaugural season in the fall of 1995.

Ruth Alexander, *above left,* the first Coordinator for Women's Athletics at the University of Florida, from 1972 to 1981 . . . Ann Marie Rogers, *above right,* who now holds that distinction, under the title of Associate Athletic Director for Women's Sports.

. . . the rest is history.

In 1973 Mimi Ryan founded the Lady Gator Invitational and nurtured the tournament to prominence on the women's intercollegiate golf circuit over the next 21 years. *Above,* freshman Riko Higashio, *on the left,* reviews her scorecard with senior All-American Dina Taylor at the 1996 Suntrust Lady Gator Invitational.

Two of the early rising stars of the Florida women's golf program: Donna Horton, twice All-State (1975, '76) and winner, *above left,* of the 1976 U.S. Golf Association Amateur championship; and Lori Gorbacz, *above right,* twice All-State (1977, '78) and All-American in 1978. Both Horton and Gorbacz went on to successful careers on the LPGA tour.

The Lady Gator golf team of 1985, NCAA champions by a resounding 15 strokes over a field of 18 at New Seabury, Massachusetts. *Above right,* Laurie Rinker, two-time All-American at Florida (1980, '82) and Lynn Connelly, *left,* 1981 SEC medalist . . . both now on the LPGA circuit.

Lady "Gator Great" Mimi Ryan, a major moving force behind the women's inter-collegiate athletic program at the University of Florida. She founded the Lady Gator golf program and watched over it for a quarter of a century, earning National Coach of the Year honors in 1986 and coaching 25 All-American selections — including four SEC Players of the Year — who brought home 11 state champi-onships, six SEC titles and two NCAA crowns.

The Lady Gator golf team of 1986, which brought another NCAA title back to Gainesville and had the rare distinction of having all five members earn All-American accolades, including '86 NCAA women's medalist Page Dunlap, *right front*.

A grateful Deb Richard, *above right,* the first Florida women's golfer to break the million-dollar mark for career winnings on the LPGA tour. She was an All-American at UF in 1984 and again in 1985.

The 1980 tennis team, *above*, found itself out in the cold — literally — in Provo Canyon, Utah (skiing, anyone?) during a regular season trek out West. By season's end they were basking in the sunshine of the first of three consecutive SEC tennis titles for UF, setting the tone for the Lady Gators' domination of the SEC in the years since — 14 league crowns in 17 years.

Above right, Jill Hetherington, four-time SEC singles champion and four-time All-American, 1984, '85, '86 and '87; *above center*, Shaun Stafford, twice an All-American at UF (1987, '88) and "Queen of the Collegiate Courts" in 1988 as NCAA women's champ; *above left*, Andrea Farley, three-time All-American (1990, '91 and '93) and a fierce competitor who epitomized the Lady Gator fighting spirit during her playing days at Florida.

In 1985 Andy Brandi took over as Lady Gator tennis mentor, and in the ensuing years, he took the program to new heights . . . up, and up, and up, to the top of the women's intercollegiate tennis world. Brandi's 1992 team, above, was 30-0 on the year (14-0 in the SEC, earning UF's seventh conference crown in Brandi's eight years at the helm) and capped their climb to the top with an NCAA team championship and individual honors for Lisa Raymond, the first of two consecutive NCAA singles title for her.

The Lady Gators continued their winning ways on the tennis courts following their 1992 NCAA championship. UF added three more SEC crowns to its coffers over the next four years and returned to the top of the ladder in 1996 with a second national championship at the '96 NCAA Women's Tennis Tournament, *top,* hosted by Florida State in Tallahassee. All the sweeter. Senior All-American Jill Craybas savored the moment, *left*.

In 1982 the inaugural NCAA Women's Swimming and Diving Championships were hosted by Florida at the O'Connell Natatorium. And when the competition was over, the National Championship trophy stayed, to become a permanent part of UF's athletic treasure trove. The Lady Gators, *above,* splashed to victory in 13 meet events on their way to that NCAA title, with sophomore Kathy Treible capturing three individual titles and being in on two relay firsts. Junior Amy Caulkins brought home a first in the 100-meter freestyle. And her little sister, a freshman named Tracy, did her part . . . adding five individual titles to the Lady Gators' total; a pretty good start for a new kid on her way to swimming immortality.

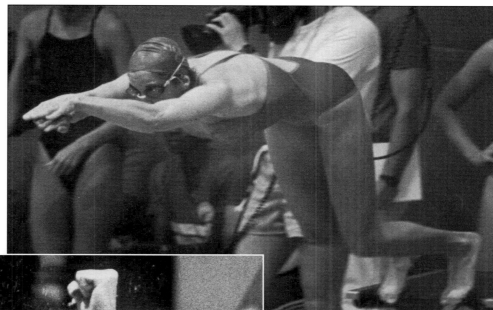

Carmen Cowart, *top,* came off the blocks to help Florida capture the 1986 NCAA 400-meter freestyle relay. Teamming with her was Mary Wayte, *above left,* who'd captured a gold medal at the 1984 Olympics in the 200-meter freestyle and would take eight NCAA titles during her Florida career (1984-88). Also on that '86 400-meter relay team was Dara Torres, *on the right,* with future Florida great Nicole Haislett. Torres would claim nine individual NCAA titles and earn 28 All-American honors during her years at UF (1985-89) and would team with Haislett on the U.S. National Team at the 1992 Barcelona Olympics.

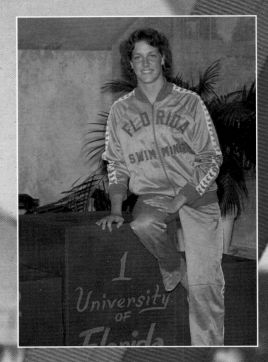

Tracy Caulkins, arguably the greatest women's swimmer of all time. In her three years at UF, from 1982 to 1984, Caulkins captured 16 NCAA titles, was honored as the National Women's Intercollegiate Swimmer of the Year in 1982, '83 and '84 and — in 1982 and '84 — received the Broderick Cup as the nation's top Female Athlete of the Year. At the 1984 Los Angeles Olympics she took three gold medals, in the 200 and 400 meter individual medleys and the 400-meter medley relay.

Gator Greats" and U.S. Olympians all: *left,* 1988 Olympian Paige Zemina, with UF and three-time Olympic swim coach Randy Reese; *below right,* Ashley Tappin, who brought home the gold in the 400-free relay at Barcelona in 1992; and, *below left,* Florida's latest Olympian, 1996 Atlanta competitor Allison Wagner, a Gainesville hometown product.

Lady Gators, *en masse*, in Barcelona at the 1992 Olympic Games: *left to right,* Beth Hazel, Janie Wagstaff, Barbara Franco and Nicole Haislett.

Gymnastics. Power and precision defined. And the Lady Gator gymnasts have fit the definition well from the very beginning of the sport in 1972-73. The 1982 team, *inset,* won an AIAW national championship, with Lynn McDonnell taking the balance beam individual. Many a brilliant performer would follow.

Maria Anz, *above left,* the picture of poise and grace, took individual honors in the floor exercise at the 1984 NCAA National Championships. Elfi Schlegel, *top right*, now an Olympic gymnastics color commentator for NBC, was brilliant in Florida's drive to the NCAA Southeast Region team championships in 1984 and '85, sweeping every event title in '84 and capturing 12 regional titles, all totalled. And Pam Titus, *bottom right,* proved to be perfection in motion, literally, during her collegiate career at Florida. She became the first collegiate gymnast to score a perfect 10.0 in floor exercise in a dual meet with Auburn in 1991, capping a four-year, three-time All-American career.

In recent years gymnastics has been a big draw and a crowd pleaser worldwide, and such is the case at Florida. On the night of February 10, 1989, a crowd of 10,651 in the O'Connell Center, *above,* watched UF defeat defending NCAA champion Alabama. It was the largest crowd ever to witness a women's athletic event in the State of Florida.

A wonderful collection of gymnastic talent: *below, left to right,* Erika Selga, Kristen Guise, Colleen Johnson and Amy Myerson, in triumph in 1995. Johnson highlighted her Florida career (1992-95) with All-American honors in the uneven bars in 1993; Guise, a Coral Springs, Florida, product, set UF records for the uneven bars (9.95) and all-around (39.65) in 1995; and Myerson earned All-American honors in three of her four years as a Lady Gator gymnast, 1993-96.

Lady Gator track came out of the starting blocks in 1972-73, with cross-country close behind during the 1973-74 school year. And it didn't take long for Heidi Hertz, *far right*, to hit winning form at the national level by taking the 1976 AIAW pentathlon crown. In cross-country Shelly Steely, leading the pack, along with teammate Donna Campbell *(above, to the left),* was 1984 SEC champion, a five-time All-American during her career at Florida (1981-85) and a 1992 Olympic performer. And the foursome of Chris Crowther, Susan Nash, Sonja Braasch and Sandra Braasch, *right, left to right,* posted a then world-record time of 8:29.35 at the 1986 Florida Fast Times meet and brought home the 3,200-meter relay crown from the '86 NCAA Championships at season's end.

The University of Florida's O'Connell Center Indoor Track has been called one of the finest and fastest indoor tracks in the nation, and the 1992 Lady Gator track team proved to be one of the finest and fastest in the nation, capturing the NCAA women's indoor track-and-field championship. Anita Howard, *left*, took first place in the 400-meters at the 1992 NCAA outdoor championships. Her list of laurels included three SEC titles from 1989 to '92 and 17 All-American citations, by far the highest total of All-American citations for any Lady Gator trackster.

INDIANA HOOSIER DOME

Michelle Freeman hurdled to victory in the 100-meters at the 1992 NCAA outdoors in Austin, Texas, *below,* and Leah Kirklin, competing at the Penn Relays, *left,* leaped to victories in the triple jump at the 1991 and '92 NCAA indoor championships and at the 1992 outdoor nationals. Another high-flying Lady Gator, Monifa Taylor, *above,* took first in the 55-meter hurdles at the 1993 NCAA indoors at the Hoosier Dome in Indianapolis.

The opening jump for Lady Gator basketball came in 1973-'74, and by the late '80s the sport was coming into its own. Sophia Witherspoon, *opposite page, top*, capped her UF career with All-SEC honors in 1991 and participated in the 1992 World University Games, as did her teammate, LaTonya McGhee, *opposite bottom,* a 1993 All-SEC selection and captain of the 1992-93 team, *above,* the first in the history of Lady Gator basketball to receive an NCAA tournament bid.

History, as they say, often repeats itself. And, happily for Florida basketball the history-making, first-ever NCAA bid of 1992-93 was repeated when the Lady Gators of 1993-94 earned another NCAA bid. The sparkplug of the '94 team was Merlakia Jones, *above,* a three-time All-SEC performer, in 1993, '94 and '95, who would conclude her career as the all-time Lady Gator scorer, with 2,001 career points.

A three-peat! The Lady Gators of 1994-95, above, the winningest team in school history, with a record of 24-9, and recipient of an unprecedented third consecutive NCAA tournament bid.

Another achievement of Olympic proportions for Florida basketball came in 1992 when former Lady Gator Tammy Jackson, *left,* became UF's first women's basketball Olympian, at the '92 Barcelona Games.

Volleyball has been a part of women's intercollegiate athletics at UF since 1974, and the Lady Gators have been serving up thrills, chills and victories in a big way in recent years. Florida came into its own in the '80s, with standouts like Lyra Vance, *below*, a first-team NCAA performer in 1987, and Connie Wolter (1987, '88), *left,* who obviously knew things were going to be okay for Florida volleyball in the years to come.

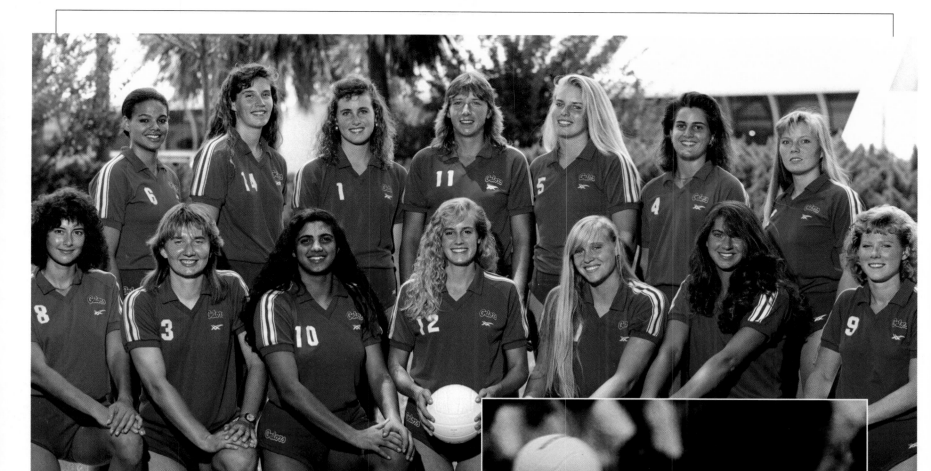

The 1991 season represented, say many, a milestone for the Lady Gators. The '91 team, above, rolled to a 35-5 record, a 13-1 conference mark and a share of the SEC regular season championship with L.S.U., whom the Lady Gators defeated in a memorable match in Gainesville during the season. The team featured All-Americans Gudula Staub, *front row, second from the left,* and Heidi Anderson, *at the right in the second row.* In 1992 Aycan Gokberk, *right,* entered school at UF and inherited the All-American mantels worn by Staub and Anderson, and the Lady Gators continued their winning ways . . . in a big way.

In the fall of 1995 the lastest addition to the Lady Gator family was born: soccer. Florida took to the field for the first time in soccer on September 2, 1995, *above,* appropriately enough against archrival Florida State. On hand for the history-making inaugural game was University president John Lombardi, *opposite page, top right,* with UF athletic director Jeremy Foley. And there was much joy in Gainesville as the Lady Gators booted FSU, 7-1. *Bottom, opposite page,* Florida's Aimee Wagstaff, *on the left,* Erin Baxter, *right,* and Jessica Fraser, *in the background,* celebrate a Gator goal.

THE EIGHTIES & NINETIES

Women's soccer is the latest, and a most welcomed addition to the sporting scene at UF's Percy Beard Stadium, where Lady Gator tracksters and their Gator brethren have long reigned supreme, a fact to which Torrance Zellner, *left,* bears witness. Zellner is the latest in a long line of Gator track and field greats, an All-American performer in 1993 and the school record holder in the 400-meter hurdles (:48.97). Another member of that long line of "Gator Greats," Scott Dykehouse, *inset left,* was the 1975 NCAA javelin champion.

Keith Brantly, *right,* one of UF's most versatile performers . . . an All-American in indoor and outdoor track and cross-country, and three times All-SEC (1981, '82, '83). Mike Blaney, *right,* twice All-SEC in cross-country (1984, '85) and All-American in 1986.

Quite a pair, Gator twins Dennis and Denise Mitchell. Denise was a three-time All-American during her career at Florida and was a member of the U.S. National Team at the World Championships in 1987. Dennis was a three-time Olympian, representing the United States in 1988 and 1992 and at the 1996 Atlanta Games. He garnered a men's school-record 12 All-American honors from 1987 to 1989, including the 1988 NCAA indoor 200-meter crown, the 1989 NCAA outdoor 200-meters and the UF 4 x 400-meter relay at the 1988 NCAA indoor championships.

Above left, eight-time All-American Tyrone Kemp, who captured the 400-meter and helped Florida bring home a first in the 4 x 400-meter relay at the 1989 NCAA indoor championships; below left, Mark Everett, a two-time Olympian (in 1988 and '92) and five-time SEC indoor champion, with nine All-American honors to his credit, including the 1990 NCAA indoor and outdoor 800-meter titles.

Above, the relay team of Dedric Jones, Lewis Lacy, Stephen Adderley and Dan Middleman took the 1992 SEC 4 x 800 title. Middleman, an accomplished distance runner, owns the school record in the 5,000-meter steeplechase (13:51.30) while Tom Nohilly, inset, *opposite page,* owns the school 3,000-meter steeplechase record (8:38.92) . . . and the 1989 NCAA crown in that event. Scott Peters, *opposite page,* teamed with Jones, Lacy, and Adderley to capture the 1992 NCAA indoor 4 x 800 relay in an American record time of 7:18.23.

An All-SEC selection in cross-country in 1983 and '84, John Rogerson, *above left,* made his mark at Florida athletically. And he made his mark in the grade-book, as an Academic All-American in 1985, as did football's Carlos Alvarez, *top right,* an All-American wide receiver in 1969 and Academic All-American. Alvarez, now a Tallahassee attorney, was voted into the GTE Academic All-American Hall of Fame in 1989. John J. Tigert, *inset right*, president of the University from 1928 to 1947, would have approved of the combination of athletic and academic excellence demonstrated by so many UF student-athletes through the years. Tigert, a football standout at Vanderbilt and a College Football Foundation Hall of Famer, received a Rhodes Scholarship to study at Oxford and took a law degree from the venerable English institution in 1907. Florida quarterback Bill Kynes, *inset left*, followed in Tigert's footsteps as a Rhodes Scholarship recepient in 1977.

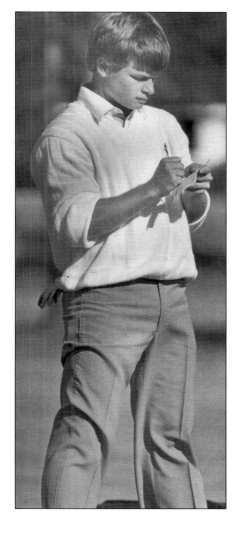

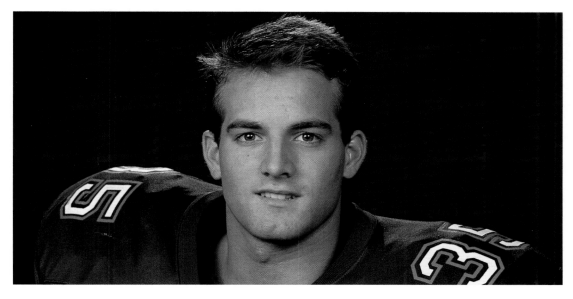

A number of other Gator gridders have distinguished themselves on the playing field and in the classroom, among them wide receiver Gary Rolle (1982-84), *top right,* and Mike Gilmore (1991-94), *bottom left,* both of whom were Academic All-Americans and entered medical school at Florida upon hanging up their cleats. All-American defensive end Brad Culpepper, *center,* was named Academic All-American, National Football Foundation Scholar-Athlete and recipient of the Draddy Award as the nation's top student-athlete in 1991. Gymnast Janice Kerr, *top left* with Alec Kessler and SEC commissioner Roy Kramer, was named All-SEC in 1987, '88 and '89 and the SEC Scholar-Athlete of the Year in 1990. And Brian Craig, *right,* was a Gator golfer for whom the numbers added up, on the scorecard and in the report card. Craig was three-time Academic All-SEC and an Academic All-American in 1992.

A number of big hitters on the college circuit and, eventually, the PGA tour have called Florida's University Golf Club home in recent years, among them: 1979 All-SEC selection Ken Green, *top*, a 1989 Ryder Cup member, with over $3 million in PGA tour earnings; *center*, 1980 All-SEC standout Mark Calcavecchia, winner of the 1989 British Open and a three-time Ryder Cup member, with $6 million in career earnings; *bottom*, four-time All-American Dudley Hart (1987-90).

And one outstanding group of golfers called the University Golf Club home, *en masse:* the 1993 Gator golf team, which brought back to Gainesville another NCAA title, guided by National Coach of the Year Buddy Alexander.

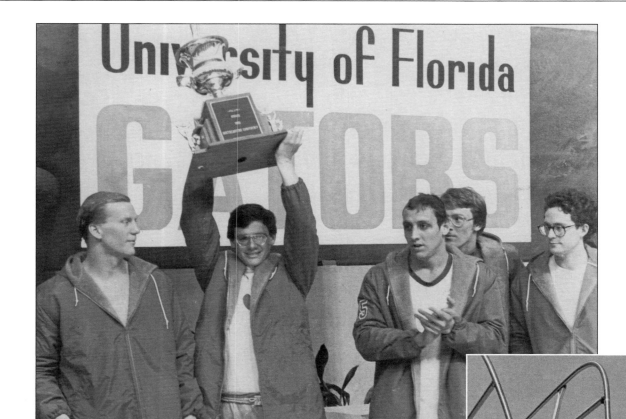

Under head coach Randy Reese, winning at Florida and championship scenes, like the one above, became routine . . . remarkably routine from 1977 to 1990. The Gators compiled a dual meet record of 100-22 during that time, captured eight SEC championships and two national championships, in 1983 and '84. And individual honors for standout performers like David Larson, *at the left with Reese in the photograph* above, were abundant. Larson took 21 All-American honors and two NCAA titles during his career (1978-81). Chris Snode, *right* with diving coach Donnie Craine, won four SEC diving titles and the 1978 NCAA 3-meter championship. He was a three-time Olympian, as well.

The Florida Gators of 1983, *top,* who captured the NCAA championship on the last event of the meet — the 400-free relay — with UF's Geoff Gaberino, Donald Gibb, Albert Mestre and Mike Heath edging out the SMU 400-free relay team, anchored by Steve Lundquist, to bring home the title. Gaberino was a member of four NCAA relay championship teams at Florida from 1981 to 1984 and won a gold medal at the 1984 Los Angeles Olympics as a member of the U.S. 800-free relay team. Heath, a four-time NCAA champion during his days at UF (1983-86), took three gold medals at the '84 Games, in the 400- and 800-freestyle and the 400-medley relay. And Mestre, who swam for his native Venezuela in the 1980 and '84 Olympics, earned 17 All-American honors and three NCAA titles while at Florida, from 1983 to 1986.

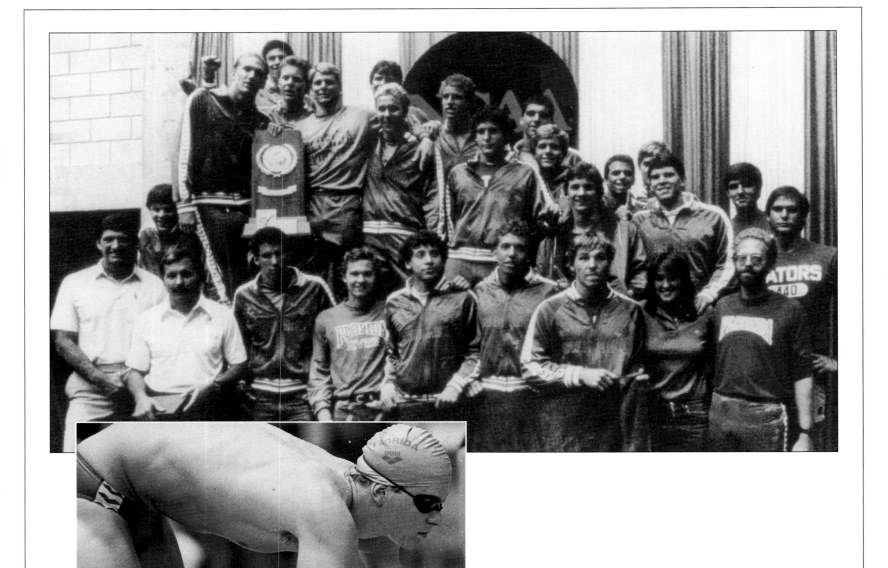

In 1984 Florida again captured the NCAA men's championship, *above,* and again it was in the last event — the 400-free relay — that the Gators were able to put enough points on the board to nail down the victory. Geoff Gaberino, Albert Mestre and Mike Heath, *inset*, teammed up with Donald Gibb this time to bring in a second-place finish in the 400 and enough points to edge out Texas, 287.5-277.

Throughout the rest of the '80s and on into the '90s there was no end to the heroes and heroics in Florida swimming. Sandy Goss, *above,* and Bob Utley, *right,* were two of the most honored swimmers in UF history. Goss garnered three SEC titles and 23 All-American honors from 1987 to 1990 and helped Florida to victory in the 1987 NCAA 800-free relay. Utley was awarded All-American accolades 22 times from 1989 to 1992 and was on UF's 1991 NCAA 400-medley relay championship team.

The story of swimming at Florida is that of an awesome aggregate collection of talent, and such is the case with the trio at left. Greg Burgess, *on the left,* was a 1992 Olympian and the 1993 NCAA Men's Swimmer of the Year, taking firsts in the NCAA 200- and 400 individual medleys in '93 and '94. Martin Zubero, *center,* was NCAA Men's Swimmer of the Year in 1991 with eight SEC titles, four NCAA titles and 15 All-American honors to his credit from 1988 and 1991. Anthony Nesti, *on the right,* is Florida's all-time leading NCAA individual champion, with five NCAA titles to his credit and 16 All-American citations between 1990 and 1992.

Since 1985 Andy Brandi has headed up the women's tennis program at Florida, and Ian Duvenhage has directed the fortunes of the Gator men's netters since 1989. The two programs, with a plethora of All-SEC and All-American selections between them, have brought back 11 SEC titles and two national championships to Gainesville. Duvenhage's 1994 crew, *above,* celebrates its SEC title.

Two in the Florida men's and women's tennis parade of national champions during the 1990s were David Blair and Mark Merklein, *left,* who took the 1993 NCAA men's doubles title. Merklein followed up with the NCAA singles crown in 1994.

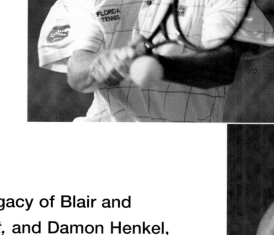

Following the championship legacy of Blair and Merklein, Dyllan Fitzgerald, *right,* and Damon Henkel, *above,* were the first players in the history of Gator men's tennis to be named All-Americans as sophomores, both in that SEC championship season of 1994.

The Gator cagers of 1969 blazed a trail from the Florida fens to New York's Madison Square Garden and the National Invitation Tournament, and the Gators of '86, *above,* won their way back to the "Big Apple" and the NIT's championship round-of-four . . . a fact that guard Ronnie Montgomery, *right,* happily acknowledged to the crowd in the O'Connell Center following UF's third-round victory over Southwest Missouri. Two cogs in the machinery that put the Gators on the road to New York were the Lawrence brothers, *left,* Pat and Joe, out of Crestview (Fla.) High School. Both were forwards, and Joe co-captained the '86 UF team, as he would the '87 crew which compiled a 23-11 record and earned Florida its first NCAA post-season tournament bid.

Florida basketball was flush with success in the mid-'80s, with NIT and NCAA bids and back-to-back 23-win seasons in 1987 and '88 — the winningest teams, to that point, in school history. The Gators were in the clouds . . . none higher than three-time All-SEC guard Vernon Maxwell, *above left*. With solid performers on hand like 1987 All-American freshman forward Livingston Chatman, *right,* the future looked bright . . .

Florida, still flying high, reached a distant and theretofore unattainable star in 1989: the SEC regular season basketball championship. The talented starting five — forwards Livingston Chatman and Dwayne Davis, guards Clifford Lett and Renaldo Garcia, and center Dwayne Schintzius — and a strong supporting cast methodically worked their way through the season and clinched the SEC title with a 104-95 victory over LSU at Baton Rouge. A deliriously happy throng turned out at the Gainesville airport, at 2:00 a.m., to greet the returning champions, a long time coming. Team captain and play-maker Clifford Lett, *above*, was among the returning heroes that night, and the Gators were champions . . .

. . . but even as the Gators basked in the sunshine of their 1989 SEC success, clouds were gathering on the horizon. An NCAA investigation of the Florida basketball program under Norm Sloan, *opposite page*, with All-American center Dwayne Schintzius, brought probation and forfeiture of the hard-won SEC crown. In due time Sloan, the talented-but-oft-troubled Schintzius and the 1989 SEC regular season title were gone, but the memories of the '89 team's accomplishments on the court remained.

The men's basketball program at Florida, filled with promise on the court and plagued with problems off, passed into new hands in the fall of 1990 . . . the guiding, motivating hands of Lon Kruger, *below,* with sophomore forward Stacey Poole. Soon, the Gator cagers were flying high again . . . and headed in a positive direction. Florida went from a 7-21 record in 1990 to 11-17 in '91 — Kruger's first year at the helm — and 19-14 in 1992. And Stacey Poole, plagued with several serious injuries during the course of his career, overcame great odds — like the Florida basketball program — to come back and wind up on top: All-SEC in 1993.

A player who, in many ways, was the quintessence of Florida basketball in the early '90s and the heart and soul of the Gator's resurgence was guard Craig Brown, *above*, Lon Kruger's first signee upon his arrival at UF. Brown, a deadeye three-point shooter, helped Florida take dead aim on returning to the upper echelon of SEC basketball . . . indeed, the upper echelon of college basketball, period. On the way to the top, in the summer of 1991, Brown helped the USA to win a gold medal at the Junior World Championships. And in 1994, behind the inspired play of team captain Craig Brown, Florida found itself back on top.

The 1994 season was the greatest in Gator cage history and the memories already the stuff of legend among the Florida faithful. It was the winningest season ever at UF — 29 wins against but 8 losses — and the Gators earned a share of first place in the SEC Eastern Division. Above all, the Gators earned an NCAA tournament bid at season's end and a first-ever trip to the NCAA Final Four in Charlotte, via Miami and the Eastern Regionals. Three-point king Craig Brown and scoring ace Dan Cross, *left*, helped Florida gun down Boston College, 74-66, in the Eastern Regionals finals at the Miami Arena, and All-SEC center Andrew DeClercq helped cut down the nets, *above* . . . and it was on to Charlotte and the "Big Dance."

The 1994 NCAA Final Four,
Charlotte Coliseum, Charlotte, NC.
And the Gators were there.

The big dance, the big leagues. The Gators have been there . . . in basketball, baseball; you name it. Many an ace has sparkled on the diamond at Florida and in the major leagues thereafter, among them Marc Sullivan, *right,* an All-American catcher at UF in 1979 and a Boston Red Sox from 1982 to 1986. Gator hurler Rob Murphy (1979-80), *above left,* proved to be one of Florida's most durable pro players, with more than a decade in the majors.

Another "Gator Great" who proved to be most durable and much-lauded in the major leagues was Florida second baseman Robby Thompson, *left*. Like Rob Murphy, Thompson logged more than a decade in the pros, and won a Golden Glove Award in 1993, *inset*, for his outstanding defensive play with the San Francisco Giants.

Infielder Herbert Perry, *right*, began and ended his career at Florida with trips to the College Baseball World Series, in 1988 and 1991, and he made his major league debut in 1994 with another World Series-bound crew, the Cleveland Indians, who captured the 1995 American League pennant and met Atlanta in the '95 World Series.

From 1982 to 1985 Scott Ruskin, *above right,* pitched 'em and Mike Stanley, *on the left,* caught 'em, and Florida bagged two SEC titles in the bargain. At the end of the '85 season, both of the dynamic duo got the call in the pro draft, Ruskin from Cleveland and Stanley from the Texas Rangers. Stanley broke into the majors with Texas in '86 and rode with the Rangers until 1992 when he traded his spurs for pinstripes, New York Yankees' pinstripes, *left.*

Florida sent one of its baseball bests — Mike Stanley — to New York in 1992. But New York had already sent its best to Gainesville. The Yankees came to town in 1987 for an exhibition match with the Gators. *Left to right,* Florida athletic director Bill Arnsparger, University president Marshall Criser and Yankees owner George Steinbrenner enjoy a moment before the game.

UF president John Lombardi, on the left, with Lylah and "Red" Barber before the 1990 Florida-Tennessee football game at which Barber, a Florida alumnus, was honored.

Long before Mike Stanley went up to New York or the Yankees came to Gainesville, UF sent one of its sons — and a man who would become a national treasure — to the Bronx and Yankee Stadium, via Cincinnati and Brooklyn. Walter Lanier "Red" Barber began his broadcasting career as a student radio announcer for the University's WRUF, calling the first game ever played at Florida Field — Florida vs. Alabama — on November 8, 1930. From those humble beginnings and his undergraduate days at Florida, Barber made his break into the major leagues in 1934 as the play-by-play man for the Cincinnati Reds. He left Cincinnati for Brooklyn and the Dodgers in 1939 and broadcast the games of the "Boys of Summer" over the next 14 seasons, until 1954, when he moved crosstown to become the voice of the New York Yankees, securing his place in the pantheon of broadcasting immortals. Barber retired in 1966, first to Miami and then Tallahassee, the latter a homecoming, of sorts, for his wife Lylah, a graduate of Florida State College for Women (now Florida State University). The two met in 1929, while "Red" was in school at UF and Lylah was a nurse at the University Infirmary, and married the following year . . . the beginning of a life-long love affair for a man whom the American sporting public admired and loved for a lifetime. While Barber was with Brooklyn, Dodgers' manager Leo Durocher made his infamous utterance, "Nice guys finish last," to the "Ol' Redhead." Happily, "Red" proved Durocher wrong, for "Red" Barber was a nice guy who finished first in the hearts of those who knew and loved him and the millions who admired him and hung on his every word from the other side of the broadcast microphone.

HAN STADIUM-PERRY FIEL

| BALL 0 | STRIKE 0 | OUT 1 |

BAT	1	2	3	4	5	6	7	8	9	10	R	H	E
FURMAN	0	0	0	0	0	0	0	0	0		0	0	0
FLORIDA	0	0	0	0	0	0	0	0	2		2	7	1

No
Hitter!! _

The heroes and the hustlers: Gator pitcher Marc Valdes, *above*, a 1992 baseball Olympian. And Gainesville hometown boy Brian Duva, *right,* two-time Academic All-SEC and Florida's "Mister Hustle" from 1991 to 1994.

Great pitching has always been a hallmark of Gator baseball, and John Burke, *opposite page,* All-SEC and All-American in 1991, continued that tradition during his playing days at Florida. Named MVP of the 1991 NCAA East Regional, Burke hurled a no-hitter against Furman in the opening game of that regional, *opposite page, inset,* and the Gators were on their way to the regional championship and the 1991 College Baseball World Series.

Pitcher Rob Bonanno, one of many remarkable success stories that are a part of the Florida baseball legacy. A walk-on from Tampa's Jesuit High School, Bonanno set a UF career strike-out record from 1991 to 1994 and earned All-SEC and All-American honors in 1994.

The 1996 Florida Gators, who took a share of the SEC baseball championship and headed to the College Baseball World Series . . . the latest Florida baseball success story.

Meanwhile. . .

Charley Pell oversaw Florida's football fortunes from the start of the 1979 season through the first three games of 1984. His first season was a disaster, with the Gators going winless in eleven games. But in 1980 Florida made one of the most remarkable turnarounds in the history of college football, going from 0-10-1 in 1979 to 8-4 in 1980, including a victory over Maryland in the Tangerine Bowl, *above right.* Pell, driven to succeed, coached the Gators to records of 7-5, 8-4 and 9-2-1 over the next three years and thought Florida was well on its way to being #1. But an NCAA probe into recruiting irregularities and rules infractions led to Pell's resignation early in the 1984 season, and it was left to Galen Hall, *opposite page,* to take the Gators to the top.

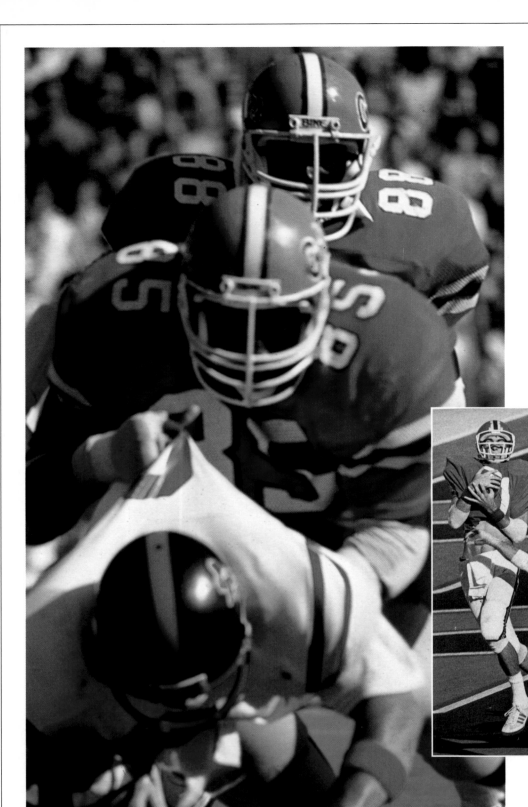

A number of "Gator Greats" distinguished themselves on the gridiron in the late '70s and '80s: *below,* wide receiver Cris Collinsworth, 1980 All-American-turned-television commentator; and David Galloway, an All-American defensive end in 1981, hanging an Ole Miss ball-carrier out to dry, *left.*

Inside the Sports Illustrated cover:

Sports Illustrated

SEPTEMBER 13, 1982 $1.50

THE PEACE CORPS

Quarterback Wayne Peace
Leads Florida Over Miami

Wayne Peace, *inset,* became Florida's starting quarterback as a freshman, midway through the 1980 season, and over the next three and a half seasons would be instrumental in the Gators' football turnaround. Wilbur Marshall, *above,* specialized in turning opponents upside-down. Marshall, a two-time All-American at linebacker (1982, '83) was the 1983 National Defensive Player of the Year.

The 1984 Florida Fighting Gators won the school's first-ever SEC football championship on the field, but in the record book the '84 championship is "vacant." The '84 season began in the midst of a storm of controversy and an NCAA investigation of recruiting violations and rules infractions at Florida. The Gators, distracted by these off-the-field proceedings, lost to Miami and were tied by LSU in their first two games. Head coach Charley Pell resigned after the third game of the season, a 63-21 venting against Tulane, and assistant coach Galen Hall stepped in as interim head coach. What followed was one of the most dramatic stories, and seasons, in Florida football history. With a former non-scholarship walk-on named Kerwin Bell at quarterback, the Gators rolled to eight consecutive victories down the stretch. By season's end, Bell was the SEC Player of the Year, and Florida was the SEC football champion, a title it eventually had to relinquish in the wake of the NCAA investigation. But that first-ever SEC football championship had been won, and no matter what the record book said officially, the Gators were SEC champions on the field and in the hearts of the Florida faithful, a victory hard-earned and justly deserved.

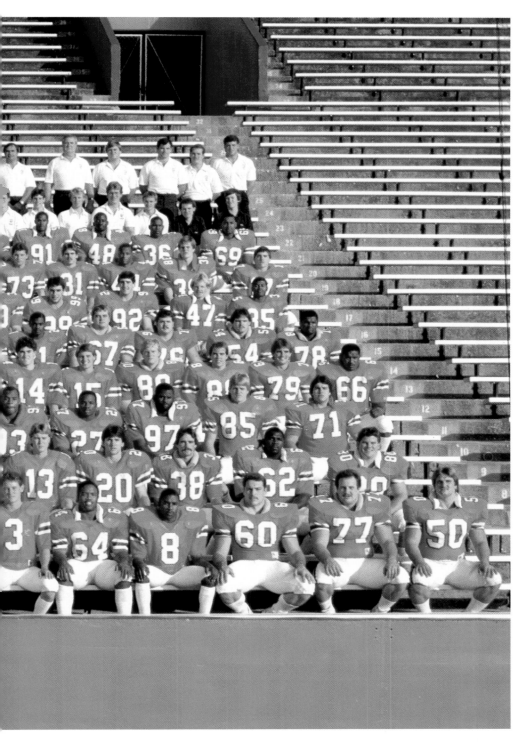

Neal Anderson, *below,* over the top and into the record books, with a school career record of 3,234 yards rushing, from 1982 to '85, and All-SEC honors in 1985.

The latter half of the 1980s represented a period of transition for Florida football after the precipitous highs and lows of the early '80s, especially the 1984 season. Quarterbacking wonder Kerwin Bell, *above right,* continued to work his magic in 1985, '86 and '87. Bell and Ricky "The Rocket" Nattiel, *above left,* teammed up for one of the most magical moments in the history of Florida football against Auburn at Gainesville in 1986. In the dying moments of the game, Bell hit Nattiel for a touchdown, then plunged over for the winning two-point conversion and a 18-17 Gator win.

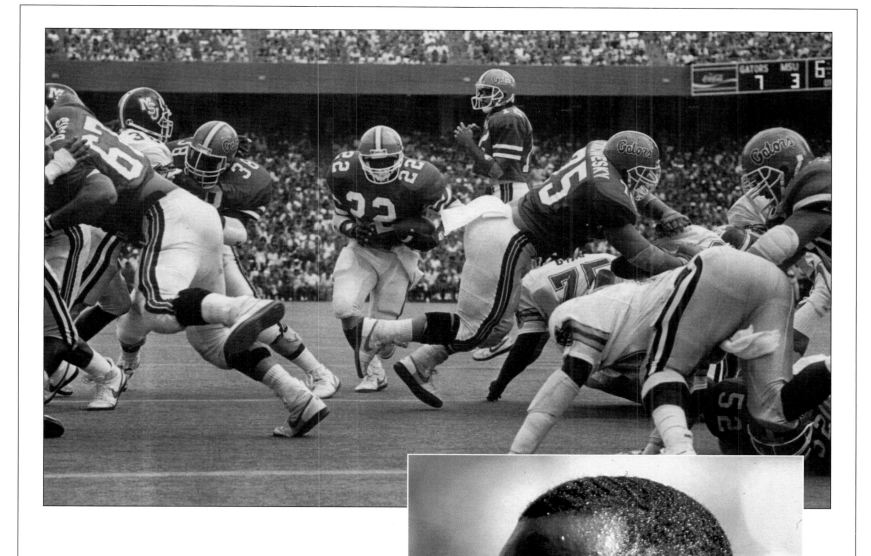

In the fall of 1987 a promising freshman running back out of Pensacola arrived on the Gainesville scene: Emmitt Smith, *right,* and *above,* taking a hand-off from then veteran quarterback Kerwin Bell in Florida's 38-3 rout of Mississippi State at Gainesville in '87. Smith went on to rewrite the Florida rushing record book and earn All-American honors in 1988 and '89.

The '80s was an era that, in many ways, typified some of the most frustrating aspects of Florida football over the years: dreams within reach that slipped away; potential that, all too often, went unfulfilled. As the decade of the '90s dawned, a couple of Gator quarterbacks — one present, one past; one in turf cleats, the other now in coaching shoes — were poised to point Florida football in an altogether different direction. Former UF All-American quarterback and 1966 Heisman Trophy winner Steve Spurrier returned to his alma mater as head coach in the spring of 1990. He observed that "we haven't accomplished all that we're capable of accomplishing in football here at Florida; haven't quite lived up to our our potential." All that was about to change. The Gators were ready to growl, and Florida fans would have much to celebrate during the decade of the '90s.

With junior Shane Matthews filling the air with passes, *left,* and deftly quarterbacking the Gators, Ben Hill Griffin Stadium saw its share of fireworks during the '91 season, and there was much cause for celebration, *above,* as Florida captured its first official SEC championship — an honor that no one and nothing could take away — in Steve Spurrier's second year. Spurrier was voted SEC Coach of the Year for the second consecutive year and Matthews the SEC Player of the Year for a second time. Matthews completed his career at Florida as the SEC's all-time leading passer, with 9,297 career yards.

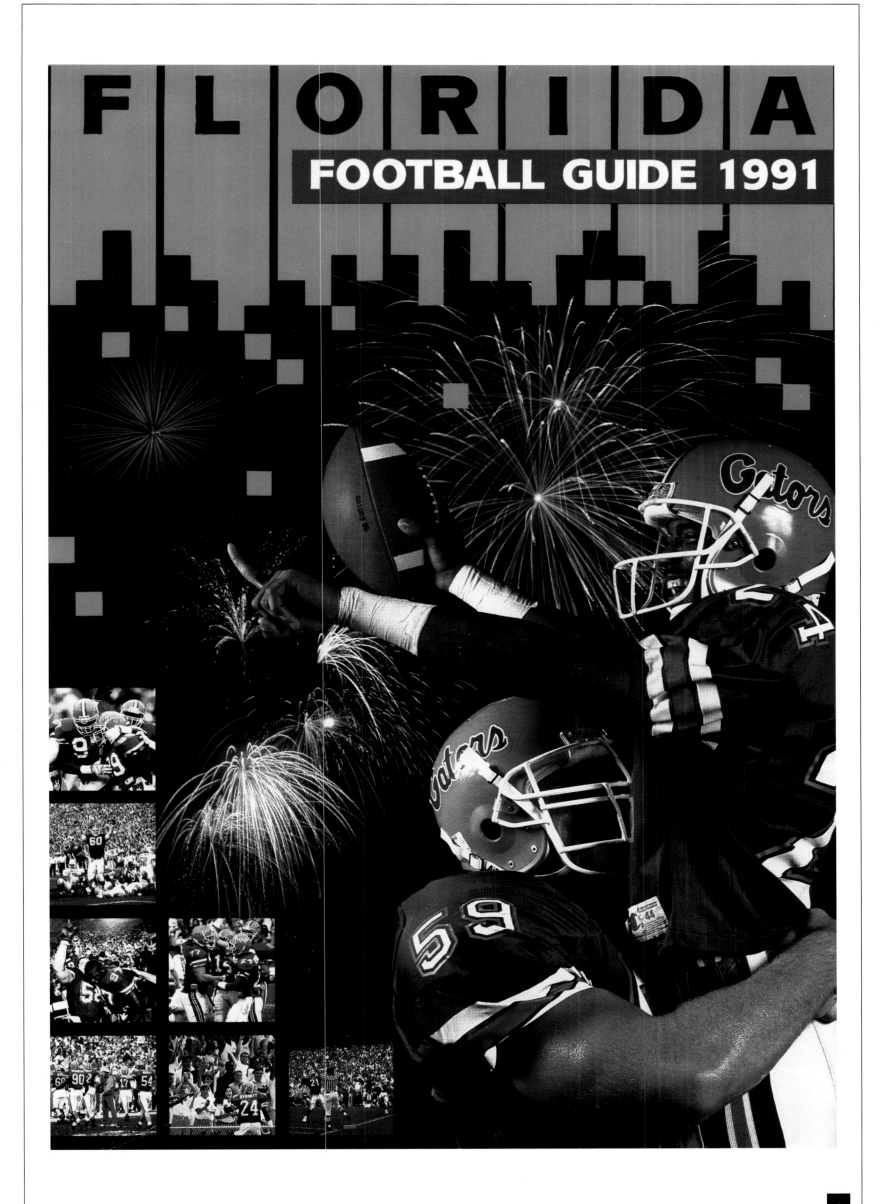

FLORIDA
FOOTBALL GUIDE 1991

Spectacular offense and solid defense earned Florida many a victory in recent years and Steve Spurrier many a victory ride. Stalwarts like defensive end Huey Richardson, *opposite page,* a 1990 All-American, kept the opposition at bay while Shane Matthews and Company lit up the scoreboards. One of the favorite sports for the Florida defense during the first half of the '90s was "Bury the Bulldog," *above.* The Gators scored six straight victories over Georgia from 1990 to 1995, and left the meter running.

S teve Spurrier nicknamed it "The Swamp," and Ben Hill Griffin Stadium at Florida Field became a riotously fun place to play, *opposite page* . . . if you were a Gator; and a down-right dangerous place to play if you weren't. If the offense didn't getcha the defense surely would. Errict Rhett, *above right*, a 1993 All-American, became UF's all-time lead-ing rusher with 4,163 yards from 1990 to 1993, eclipsing Emmitt Smith's career total . . . as the decade of the '90s, and the fun in the Florida sun, rolled on and on and on.

All-American wide receiver Jack Jackson with one of the 57 passes (15 for touchdowns) that he hauled down in 1994, en route to SEC Offensive Player-of-the Year honors.

It all began unassum-ingly enough . . . the season, and the game. Houston came to town for Florida's 1995 home opener, and the Gators found themselves behind twice in the first quarter (0-7 and 7-14) and locked in a 14-14 tie at the quarter's end. Then, UF exploded for 21 second-quarter points, a 35-14 halftime lead and cruised to a 45-21 win. A week later the Gators wal-lopped Kentucky,

42-7, on the road in a more impressive but still incon-clusive showing. Then, eighth-ranked Tennessee came to town for a showdown in "The Swamp" with #4 Florida. The Vols, a more than worthy opponent for the Gators, rolled to a 30-14 lead midway through the second quarter. Then, in one of the most stunning reversals in the history of college football, Florida — led by quarterback Danny Wuerffel — thundered to 48 straight points and a 62-37 victory. By game's end it was readily apparent that this pack of Gators was something special . . . very special. Danny Wuerffel, *above,* garnered All-American and SEC Player of the Year honors; senior Chris Doering, *opposite page, inset,* capped his career by breaking a number of Carlos Alvarez's school and SEC pass receiving records, which had stood for a quarter of a century. And the Gators roared through the regular season and the SEC Championship Game — Florida's third straight SEC championship — undefeated and untied, 12-and-oh on the year and #2 in the nation. A shootout with #1-ranked Nebraska was set up in the Fiesta Bowl to decide the National Championship, and the Cornhuskers came away with the victory. But the Fighting Gators of '96 and the wonders they wrought will be for-ever remembered in Gainesville. The stuff of legends.

NEBRASKA

VS.

FLORIDA

THE NATIONAL

CHAMPIONSHIP